BUILDING PARTNERSHIPS

Computing and Library Professionals

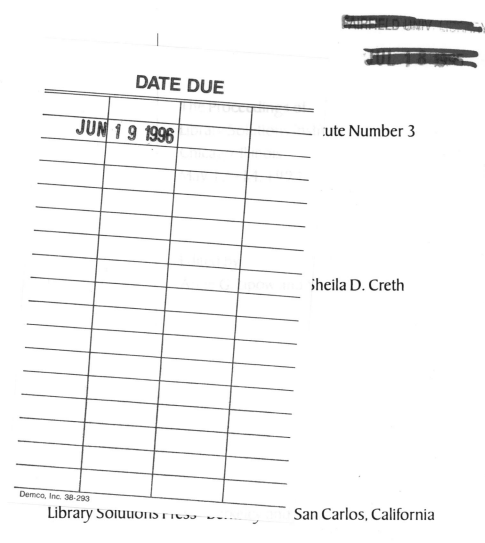

...ute Number 3

...Sheila D. Creth

Library Solutions Press — San Carlos, California

First printing: March 1995
Book design by Catherine Dinnean
Copyright © Library Solutions Press

LIBRARY SOLUTIONS PRESS

Sales Office   1100 Industrial Road, Suite 9
                                San Carlos, CA 94070

Fax orders: 415–594–0411

Telephone orders:
and inquiries: 510–841–2636

Web URL: http://www.internet-is.com/library/

Email: info@library-solutions.com

Editorial Office: 2137 Oregon Street, Berkeley, CA 94705

ISBN   1-882208-18-8

TABLE OF CONTENTS

Preface

Anne G. Lipow and Sheila D. Creth

In May 1994 a large number of library and computing professionals came together in a two-day program to explore ways to move both professional groups through the present environment of turmoil and change to a more stable future by working together in new ways. Sixty-one registrants participated in the program with fifty-five individuals attending as partners from library and computing centers at the same institution. The organizers of the program represented both the library and the computing portions of this partner equation: Anne Lipow, Sheila Creth, and Michael Staman.

The papers in this publication are the formal presentations that provided the framework for the discussions and deliberations that were the primary focus of the Institute. Included are contributions submitted after the Institute by participants describing collaborative projects underway on their campuses. And in a final appendix is a reprint of a paper by Sheila Creth that was a pre-Institute reading assignment for the participants to suggest a focus as they began their work together.

What does not, cannot, appear in this publication is the full flavor of the discussions and the many issues that emerged from the participant interactions. Nor is there any way to adequately describe the energy and commitment that the participants brought to exploring both the need and the challenges of working together more effectively.

Program Content

Highlights of the program following the speakers is provided for individuals who may want to initiate a similar program between computing and library professionals in their organization.

Small Group and Plenary Discussions

The following provides a summary of some perspectives and ideas that emerged from the small group and plenary discussions.

Both computing and library participants used these terms to describe their own professions:

- provide access to information
- assess available information resources
- integrate resources
- instruct in how to use information-retrieval tools
- manage information resources
- identify appropriate resources/tools
- support the campus mission

They see their primary differences in how they implement these activities:

- Library professionals are responsible for providing the infrastructure that links the <u>content</u> of the information resources;
- Computing professionals are responsible for the physical, technological infrastructure that <u>transmits</u> the information resources.

The professional groups overlap in some functions such as:

- store, retrieve, and manage information
- deliver information
- establish and manage networks, on campus and between the campus and external locations
- train constituencies in aspects of computer and information literacy

The professional groups consider their unique roles to be in the following areas:

Computing professionals

- handle large-scale computing
- establish campus-wide standards for hardware and software
- ensure security of network
- maintain and upgrade network capacity
- provide gateways, support computer software, and provide expertise in programming

Library professionals
- identify, evaluate, acquire, organize, and describe information resources in all formats
- instruct in use of all information resources
- instruct in network use and multimedia systems
- preserve information resources
- ensure continuity and stability of resources—print and electronic

Each defined the **other profession's** role more narrowly:
- Computing professionals described the librarian's role as centering around cataloging and managing print collections;
- Library professionals described the computing person's job as centering around the management of technical support for mainframe systems and networks.

Ice Breaker

It wasn't far into the first morning before the basis of potential clashes was out in the open. Unscheduled in the formal agenda but emerging almost accidentally from a discussion regarding the similarities and differences between the two professions, a frank airing of stereotypes each profession holds of the "other" took place. Here are some of the attitudes that were expressed:

1. Librarians don't understand technology and never will.
2. Computer types aren't service oriented.
3. Librarians are inflexible and resist change, librarianship being an old, traditional occupation, whereas computer folks thrive on change and hate it when things are the same after six months.
4. Computing people lack a common set of values, whereas librarians live by a code of ethics.
5. Librarians like dust and mold that go with the old books.
6. Computing people don't know how to run a meeting, much less an organization.
7. Computing people like to fix things quickly; librarians deliberate over issues and problems forever.
8. Librarians work closely with their users and listen to their needs; computing professionals act as individuals and do not consider users at all.
9. Librarians are passive-aggressive.
10. Computing people are aggressive-abrasive.

This half-in-jest/half-serious banter led to the refutation of each type-cast, with the result that participants learned new information about the other group that increased mutual understanding and respect—the foundation for collaborative effort.

The formal presentations within the program focused on why it is a critical time for library and computing professionals to find common ground: on the one hand, rapid change in higher education calls into question the validity and role of each profession and, on the other hand, an acknowledgment that the combined skills of both professions are essential to address the emerging developments brought about by information technology. The small group and plenary sessions and the structured exercises resulted in a recognition regarding the interdependence of the two professions.

Following, in an outline format, are selected results of the participants' efforts.

1. In a **redesigned future**, while each profession would have its own specialized responsibilities that do not overlap, the two professions would share responsibility in the following areas:
   - training to access information
   - supporting customers
   - designing discipline-oriented systems
   - collaborating with faculty
   - writing grant applications
   - archiving information and records management
   - negotiating licensing agreements
   - integrating technology, and networked and multimedia information into the curriculum
   - designing user interface and delivery systems
   - providing 24-hour service
   - strategic planning

2. New **organizational models** that fostered collaborative activities would have the following characteristics:
   - client-centered
   - flexible, adaptable
   - self-managed teams
   - accountable for team results
   - flatter organization
   - staff training and development a priority

- strategically focused
- shared vision and values developed recognition, rewards based on new expectations

3. Examples of **partnership projects** that should be given high priority:
    - assist faculty and staff in multimedia development and use
    - provide frontline user support
    - create program for staff development
    - establish an electronic text center
    - co-locate parallel staff
    - issue publications and documentation
    - apply for grants
    - define minimum workstation equipment for information access
    - plan R & D experiments
    - reengineer human resources
    - plan space and facilities
    - experiment with mobile technologies and wireless communication

4. Next steps

In the final phase of the Institute, participants met with their home partners. Those six individuals who did not have an institution partner met together. At this final stage, participants discussed practical next steps toward accomplishing collaborative projects that they felt they could undertake upon returning home. Below are examples of their plans:

- collaborate on electronic journals and training
- spend time each week in joint planning
- develop a "hot issues" list to discuss jointly
- add representation of the "other" on existing committees
- reengineer together to build trust
- build on the existing Library-Computing Web Server
- develop CWIS as joint project
- meet together with respective "bosses" to educate them about importance of collaboration
- replicate this type of program on campus

- begin cross-functional training for front-desk staff
- improve partnering with external schools, organizations
- design cultural integration of organizations
- library and computing directors issue statement to staff regarding commitment to and expectation for collaborative efforts
- organize joint staff meetings periodically

About the Program Presenters and Facilitators

SHEILA D. CRETH is University Librarian at the University of Iowa, where she has introduced a number of innovative programs, including a state-of-the-art electronic information and learning center known as the Information Arcade. She previously held administrative positions in three university libraries and served on the administrative staff of the Columbia University Computing Center. Her recent publications and activities focus on "managing in cyberspace"—the implications of information technology on organizational structure, and on the roles and responsibilities of library and computing professionals, including their working relationships within and outside their separate departments. She serves on the EDUCOM Board of Trustees' Steering Committee for the Coalition for Networked Information and is a member of the NASULGC Commission on Information Technology.

KAY FLOWERS is Assistant University Librarian and Director of Library Technology at Rice University. As Director of Library Technology, she works with the library automation group on the continuing implementation of technology in the library, including the installation of a new library system. Her projects include working to create an electronic reserve service and working with a team to review and revise the campus copyright policy as it applies to electronic information. Kay received her BA in English, Sociology and Behavioral Science from Rice University and her MS in Library Science from the University of Illinois. She is currently completing an MA in psychology with an emphasis on human-computer interaction.

STEPHEN FRANKLIN is Director of Advanced Scientific Computing in the Office of Academic Computing and Lecturer in Information and Computer Sciences at the University of California, Irvine. He received degrees in Mathematics from Harvard College (BA) and the University of Chicago (Ph.D.) and specializes in scientific visualization, computer-assisted learning, and networked information resources.

SARA KIESLER is Professor of Social and Decision Sciences at Carnegie Mellon and is a member of the University's Robotics Institute. She is a distinguished speaker and author (including *Connections: New Ways of Working in the Networked Organization*, MIT Press, 1991). With a Ph.D. in social psychology (Ohio State University), her research centers on the effect of computer-mediated and information technology on individuals and organizations.

ANNE G. LIPOW is Director of Library Solutions Institute. She is a frequent consultant, speaker, and author in management and organizational change. She is a co-author of *Crossing the Internet Threshold: An Instructional Handbook* and Coordinating Editor of the Internet Workshop Series—all published by Library Solutions Press, Berkeley, California.

ANDREA MARTIN is Assistant Director for the Office of Computing Services at Rice University. She also heads the User Services Group, which includes consultants, trainers, technical writers, LAN specialists, reference librarians, and government publications librarians. She has a BS in Electrical Engineering and an MM in Music. She has served as co-principal investigator for a NASA trajectory operations software evaluation, research associate for an IBM-sponsored graphics project, and project manager for the Rice Macintosh Software Development Project.

E. MICHAEL STAMAN is President of CICNet, Inc. and a founder and Interim President of CoREN, Inc. His background includes over 26 years in technologies in both the higher education and private sectors; consulting, research, publications, and professional service in a variety of societies; and creator of several important Internet concepts such as Rural Datafication (sm) and Wide Area Information Resources Management (WAIRM). Dr. Staman has served on numerous boards, including his current activities as a member of the board of the Federation of American Research Networks (FARNET). One of his major interests is in how networking can best support the mission of universities.

Acknowledgement

We wish to thank the editors of *CAUSE/EFFECT* magazine for their help in editing the papers by Sara Kiesler and Kay Flowers and Andrea Martin. *CAUSE/EFFECT* published these two papers in its Fall 1994 issue.

WORKING TOGETHER APART

Sara Kiesler

Carnegie Mellon University

Today's popular and business press extols the virtues of collaboration and teamwork. Collaboration is said to increase learning, innovation, flexibility, participation, and understanding of organizational goals. Our watchwords are "interdisciplinary teams," "computer-supported collaborative work," "flat organization," "self-management," and "horizontal corporation."

I want to offer the perspective of a social scientist on collaboration, more particularly the perspective of a social scientist who studies how new information and communication technologies are changing (or not changing) the nature of collaboration. Some people feel that new technology, especially computer-based networking, fosters collaboration. Others see in information technology one more means for administrators to reduce costs, monitor performance, or impose new demands on subordinates. Still other criticize the hyperbole surrounding new technology and "new" forms of organization. At a recent seminar on quality management, one of my colleagues declared, "TQM is just another fad!" One can hardly deny that change can be a sacred belief. Sheila Creth writes that it's important to separate hyperbole from reality.[1]

The issue I address here is how it's possible for people to collaborate who are separated by department and profession, and perhaps also by geography, and whether or not technology helps.

Collaboration defined

Collaboration is, very simply, working cooperatively with others towards shared group goals. Usually collaboration implies peers who communicate directly and informally as well as in planned meetings. In most work organizations, boundary-spanning collaboration is difficult within the fundamental, vertical structure we social scientists call "hierarchy." Hierarchy encompasses the Weberian ideas of bureaucracy and chain of command.[2] Bureaucracy standardizes communication and relationships. The chain of command regulates who reports to, and depends on, whom. Within a hierarchy (vertical structure) there are departments, rules, and levels of authority that formalize boundaries and barriers between groups. Theoretically, hierarchy offers an efficient alternative to direct communication. Rather than everybody repeatedly discussing what each person should do, hierarchy allows management to distribute work and exercise control through layers of supervision, which in turn buffer managers from unnecessary communications.

Collaboration is more comfortable within another fundamental structure of organizations, the horizontal structure. Horizontal structure is the division an specialization of work along lines of expertise. Horizontal structure has always existed side by side with vertical structure and can be traced at least to the specialized craftsmen found in medieval feudal manors and monasteries and later in crafts guilds.[3] Professional, technical, and crafts people traditionally are organized horizontally, by occupation or specialization. In a horizontal structure, people work effectively because of their training and collaborations, rather than because of bureaucratic rules and management control. Figure 1 illustrates an organization's vertical and horizontal structure.

The more technical and specialized people's work becomes, the more they must collaborate. They must continually exchange specialized, substantive knowledge not just to keep up with changes in tech-

TECHNICAL WORK AND OCCUPATIONAL ALLEGIENCE

		HIGH	LOW
Formal Authority in Organization	HIGH	Managers (Level 5)	Professionals
		Managers (Level 4)	
		Managers (Level 3)	
		Managers (Level 2)	Technical Workers
		Managers (Level 1)	
	LOW	Clericals/Operatives	

FIGURE 1. Categories of workers in the vertical and horizontal organizational structure (adapted from Barley, 1994, Figure 5). Italics denote respondents in the Hinds-Kiesler study of a large telecommunications firm. Technical workers reported to managers at level 2.

niques and innovations, but also to diagnose problems and come up with solutions. Studies of scientific and technical work have long shown that coordination in those fields occurs primarily through direct communication and collaboration among different specialists.[4]

Administrators working within a vertical, hierarchical structure communicate somewhat differently and often fail to appreciate the nature of collaboration. In a recent study of ours in a large telecommunications firm,[5] we found that technical employees with equivalent seniority were less differentiated by hierarchical level than administrative employees were. They had more peer communications (over 70 percent versus 46 percent for administrators at the same level). For these peer communications, they preferred real-time interaction and thus were more likely to use the telephone (synchronous interaction) rather than asynchronous technology such as email or voice mail (38 percent versus 16 percent for administrators). We predicted that of the asynchronous technologies, voice mail would be a choice of administrators and email would be used by technical people (when synchrony wasn't possible). Both are convenient, but the voice is especially good for exerting control, whereas text is better for exchanging technical information. As we predicted, technical employees' asynchronous communications favored email over voice mail 3:1, whereas the reverse was true of administrators and of hierarchical communications. Administrators and technical employees both seemed to be unaware of how much their patterns and tastes in communication actually diverged.[6]

Organizations are changing

Collaboration and teamwork are slogans. But organizations also are exploring structures and cultures of collaboration in response to a real, long-term shift in the nature of work. Steven Barley, an ethnologist at Cornell University, says that two major forces are responsible:

(1) The growth of large corporations has created more demand for professionals.

(2) The explosion of scientific and technical knowledge, and technological change, has unleashed demand for technical work and created new technical occupations and professions.[7]

The occupations of programmer, systems analyst, operations researcher, and computer repair technician, novel in the 1960s, now employ over 1.5 million people. Crafts, professional, and technical workers were 15 percent of employed people at the turn of the century, 22 percent by 1950, 28 percent by 1991, and are forecast to be 30 percent or nearly a third of the labor force by 2005. The increasing professionalization of organizations and "technization" of work implies an increased emphasis on horizontal structure and collaborative flows of communication.

Fostering collaboration

Despite this century's romance with systematic management (hierarchy, control, bureaucracy), firms have always attempted to foster collaboration in certain areas such as R & D (research and development). Firms use at least four mechanisms to foster collaboration: (1) interdepartmental committees, (2) rotation of personnel across functions, (3) project team with cross-functional participation (a major part of TQM), and (4) computer networking, including use of email, bulletin boards, and conferencing facilities.

Data from a recent preliminary survey of large companies—ranging from dog food companies to high-tech computer companies—suggest that about half of all companies are using each approach. (This study, by Wes Cohen and John Walsh in our department at Carnegie Mellon, eventually will give a picture of how collaboration between R & D and other functions actually affects organizational performance.)

Three features of these methods are worth noting. First, each of the methods challenges the strictures of hierarchy. Second, each is boundary spanning, and maneuvers people into contact with different groups. It goes without saying that a collaboration is hardly that without ongoing communication and common work. Third, successful collaboration can be costly. James Barker's report on self-managed teams in a small telecommunications company describes a change from supervisory to participatory structures ·that involved reorganizing both work and equipment, educating and working with middle managers to move them to new "coordinator" positions, paying costs of termination of those who would not be happy in the new environment, hiring consultants, implementing extensive training for employees, developing new systems and methods for measuring problems and performance, and searching for and hiring new people with the "right" attitudes. The switch was successful and saved the company, but it didn't come free or easily.[8]

Even if mechanisms for collaboration were free, it would still be hard. Collaboration lacks the structure and rules of communication in a hierarchy. Collaboration therefore relies more than other kinds of interaction on trust and a sense of common purpose. If collaboration is to be carried out across organizational, social, and/or geographic boundaries, those boundaries can impede the development of trust.

Psychologists who study cooperation or trust enumerate at least three fundamental processes, inescapable in organizations, that make collaboration difficult: (1) social distinctions, even "irrelevant" ones, (2) wage and salary differentiation, and (3) subcultural differences. I will give an example of each, since one must be sensitive to the seeds of mistrust in order to foster collaboration.

Job and department boundaries

Laboratory studies show that even a minimal experimental procedure, such as dividing a larger group of subjects into two groups based on the color of a poker chip pulled from a hat, causes the subjects to cooperate more with in-group members (the ones with the same color chip) and to show much more competitive behavior with the out-group (the ones with the different color chip). This happens in part because of the economics of the way we think. Rather than think about people complexly, we tend to group people into categories, especially into "us" versus "them." Any dividing line between people tends to bring about a categorization of in-group and out-group. To bring two groups together one must either blur the boundaries between the groups, or create a cross-cutting category that fosters more complex thinking.[9]

Wage and salary differentiation

In the literature of both psychology and economics, there is evidence that wage dispersion negatively affects teamwork and collaboration. Wage or salary dispersion reinforces status and power differences and hierarchy. Jeff Pfeffer and Nancy Langton have shown that the greater the dispersion of wages and salaries in universities, the less people collaborate.[10] In academic departments, the greater the salary dispersion, the lower is faculty satisfaction, productivity, and likelihood of collaborating with one another.

Subculture

Subcultures stabilize groups and help people become socialized to professions, but they also increase the distance between groups. For instance, despite all the changes over the last few decades that have brought computer scientists and engineers into the real world of business and academic life, a distinctive computing subculture still sets computer professionals apart from others in the college or university. A computer scientist friend laughingly refers to his groups as "techno-weenies." Libraries also have a distinctive subculture. Sheila Creth discusses many differences between librarians and computer professionals. A demographic difference that reinforces cultural difference is that computer science remains a preserve mainly of men, and library science more of women. The demographic difference is readily visible and acts as a signal (or social context cue) of dissimilarity. Also, there are real differences in the ways men and women communicate, and in the ways they are treated by their organizations. Subculture differences can't be subordinated to "mere" sociology. Often they crop up in unlikely places, especially in ostensibly trivial discussions, like "who should be invited to the meeting."

Networks in collaboration

Networked communication remains, by a large margin, the only well-used computer-supported collaborative technology. Shared databases, intelligent agents, calendars, and so forth still don't work well enough for users to have taken them to heart. The CSCW community itself doesn't use them.[11] Also, people love to talk to other people on networks—usually more than they love to interact with a database or some other application.

Two features of network communication that are very important for collaboration are "access equalization" and "social equalization."[12]

Access equalization

Access equalization derives from people's ability to contact different people than they would have before, to form new groups, or to maintain ties that would have decayed in the past. We call this access equalization because the benefit is mainly to "peripheral" members of organizations. People at the center of an organization (the "information haves") usually have plenty of information and plenty of contact with others, whereas this is less true of people at the periphery—those who are lower in the hierarchy, geographically remote, mobile, or members of small specialized groups.

John Walsh and Todd Bayma studied scientific collaborations that use email to interact.[13] Perhaps in part because of networks, scientific collaborations are increasing. For example, in mathematics, from 1980 to 1990 the number of papers that were jointly authored jumped 33 percent. Almost all the additional collaboration were with remote colleagues. They quote one experimental particle physicist:

> There are two modes of experiments at Fermi: fixed target and collider—smashing protons and anti-protons in the accelerator ring. The fixed tend to be smaller—sixty scientists. The collider is more limited in the number of experiments that can run. The one I'm on has 200 physicists. In both cases, they're from all over. In one experiment, there is a large contingent of Italians, on a fixed garget experiment. I have colleagues from France, Russia, China, South American, and all over the U.S.

In these experiments, coordination at a distance is essential.

> We have a collaborators meeting every two months. We have 100 people there from all over the world. E-mail is essential. The success of the meeting depends on the organization and effective use of the net. The two experiments I'm on use different techniques. [In] the collision experiment they have set up a News System [an electronic bulletin board]. All collaborators except the Russians, Chinese, and Indians are on. News goes on that. Then all can access and find out. The agenda is sent around this way. We use the nets for agenda items. Weekly meetings. Make announcements. With the test beam data, we discuss procedures, data. We use it to tell someone to do this, or maybe we should get together and discuss X. That way you know ahead and can come prepared. The News is available to all. You send an announcement of a meeting and ask for input for the agenda. When you are requesting input, you will send targeted e-mail to individuals. If you are not coming, you will e-mail to the organizer in private.

> The other experiment I'm in doesn't use e-mail as effectively. It's a personal trait of the organizer. As a consequence, the collaboration is less effective. People aren't as organized. They don't know what they are supposed to do....For a collaborators meeting, I'll get a message 10:00 p.m. the night before with the agenda. There is no way to react.

A chemist said, in response to how people in his field use e-mail:

> Gossip, definitely. It's a very important component of mes-
> sages. If you only see people once a year, you need to let
> them know you care about them as a person, not just as a
> disembodied voice at the end of a phone line. Otherwise, I
> don't think you could maintain a long-distance project like
> this.

Walsh thinks of a collaboration as a set of connections that decays
over time unless occasionally activated (somewhat like neural networks). Computer network communication provides an important
mechanism for maintaining ties with others that might otherwise
decay.

Social equalization

Another feature of networks important to collaboration is a change
in group dynamics we call "social equalization." This effect comes
about primarily because communication in a network is mainly by
text. Looking at text alone, especially somewhat brief messages, we
have few social context cues that signal people's social and organization differences. All communication technologies attenuate to at
least some extent the social context cues available in face-to-face
conversation, but email does so even more than other technologies.
Our experiments and field studies suggest that, through the reduction of social context cues, people are less socially inhibited, more
open, and even more risky or unconventional in making decisions
than when they communicate in other venues. When social context
cues are missing, people can't "see" the boundaries that divide them,
so they participate more equally in group discussions, and some status differences are reduced. There is some new evidence that brainstorming electronically is more effective than brainstorming face-
to-face. When people can all type in ideas without interference, and
without fear of evaluation, they offer more ideas and more creative
ideas than in standard brainstorming sessions.

With fewer social context cues and more participation, it follows
that discussions lengthen and conflict increases as people bring out
concerns that might have kept to themselves otherwise. Accordingly,
when participation increases in electronic groups, decision-making
isn't as efficient. It takes groups longer to make decisions and to
solve problems than it would otherwise take. Hence there always is
a tradeoff necessary when you leave the predictability of standard
meetings and work in an electronic environment. People of our gen-

eration have not grown up in such an environment, and the etiquette and rules are still being worked out.

Conclusion

Collaborations are more effective when they have a synergistic effect—when the whole is more than the sum of its parts. In a successful collaboration, people can amplify each other's ideas and jointly develop a better plan than the plan of any individual. Hence it is a good idea to create an electronic or "virtual" group when, because of distance or organizational or social differences, one would otherwise have no collaboration at all. Electronic communications also work well when an existing collaboration has too little opportunity for face-to-face interaction. Electronic communication can be used to extend and cement relationships. Electronic communication can prevent dispersed groups from delegating too many decisions to a manager or to another group, and it can ensure there is input from everyone and attention to everyone's concerns. However, as the testimony from the physicist suggests, electronic groups do not work well without organization, support, and attention to the needs of members and their work. Nor are electronic meetings equivalent to face-to-face meetings. Organizations with extensive electronic communication find the role and character of collaborations are changing, but electronic communication will never automate trust.

Notes

1. S. D. Creth, "Creating a Virtual Information Organization: Collaborative Relationships Between Libraries and Computing Centers," *Journal of Library Administration* 19 (1993): 111-132.

2. M. Weber, *Economy and Society* (Berkeley, Calif.: University of California Press, 1968/1922).

3. A. Kieser, "Organizational, Institutional, and Societal Evolution: Medieval Craft Guilds and the Genesis of Formal Organizations," *Administrative Science Quarterly* 34 (1989): 540-564.

4. T. J. Allen, *Managing the Flow of Technology* (Cambridge, Mass.: MIT Press, 1977); and J. Lave, "Situating Learning in Communities of Practice," in L.B. Resnick, J. M. Levine, and S. D. Teasley (eds.), *Perspectives on Socially Shared Cognition* (Washington, D.C.: American Psychological Association, 1988), pp. 63-84.

5. P. Hinds and S. Kiesler, *Vertical and Horizontal Structures Enacted in the Use of New Communication Technologies* (Pittsburgh, Pa.: Carnegie Mellon University, 1994).

6. People were also unaware of how their own perspectives on communication changed depending on their position. One manager complained bitterly about the voice mail system in his firm that cut him off before he had finished giving instructions to subordinates. "I need to give important instructions using the technology, and it doesn't let me. You get cut off after three minutes." At the end of our interview, I asked the manager if he wished to make any other comments. "Yes," he said, "I really hate how people leave long messages on voice mail."

7. S. Barley, *The Turn to a Horizontal Division of Labor: On the Occupationalization of Firms and the Technization of Work*, Philadephia, Pa: National Center for the Educational Quality of the Workforce, University of Pennsylvania, 1994).

8. J. H. Barker, "Tightening the Iron Cage: Concertive Control in Self-managing Teams," *Administrative Science Quarterly* 38 (1993): 408-437.

9. A conference participant offered the example of a picnic that his management gave to bring together two departments. It organized a volley ball game between teams representing each department, but the game just exacerbated competitive feelings between the departments. The participant said, "It was a big mistake." But when the teams were mixed up and composed of people from each department, it changed the whole tenor of the picnic.

10. J. Pfeffer and N. Langton, "The Effect of Wage Dispersion on Satisfaction, Productivity, and Working Collaboratively: Evidence from College and University Faculty," *Administrative Science Quarterly* 38 (1993): 382-407.

11. CSCW refers to computer-supported cooperative work. Anthropologist Diana Forsythe, who studies the artificial intelligence community, says AI researchers hardly ever study actual users or visit their work settings. Hence, it isn't surprising that AI continues to develop applications that "users" don't use.

12. For a technical review of this research, see S. Kiesler and L. Sproull, "Group Decision Making and Communication Technology," *Organizational Behavior & Human Decision Processes* 52 (1992): 96-123.

13. J. Walsh and T. Bayma, *Social Structure and Technology: Computer Networks and Scientific Work* (Chicago: University of Illinois at Chicago Circle, 1993).

ORGANIZATION DESIGN: NEW PATHS FOR COLLABORATION

Sheila D. Creth
University of Iowa

Introduction

All organizations are in a period of transformation including universities with information technology acting as both a catalyst and an instrument of change. Indeed information technology promises to be one of the more powerful influences in shaping higher education into the 21st century. Librarians and computer professionals working as partners can be major players in the innovative application of these technologies in support of the university's mission. But to achieve this requires that they consider opportunities and options for collaboration, along with ways that the organization structure and culture will need to change to support collaboration in an environment of rapid and pervasive change.

It is clear that the librarians and computing professionals need to imagine and explore new models for interaction and integration of activities and support. Their attention, or concern, should no longer be focused on administrative merger; this may or may not happen depending on the local campus environment. Instead recognition of the interdependence of both organizations and the professionals in each should generate a desire to identify new ways of working together and creating new opportunities for applying the collective efforts of both. The integration of information technology into all aspects of teaching, learning and research activities suggest an urgency to examining opportunities for new relationships among library and computing professionals. Specifically, librarians and technologists should be working collaboratively on such activities as strategic planning, designing campus networks and technological infrastructure along with broad-based information and knowledge management systems, developing campus information policies, designing instructional programs, and supporting curriculum development by faculty. These are distinctly different activities than ones in which the library and computing professionals have worked together in the past and a different approach than what was used in the past is required. Computing and library professionals need to create a truly collaborative culture in which they work together to develop mutual goals and projects that will benefit the university community.

Schrage, in his book *Shared Minds: The New Technologies of Collaboration,* defines collaboration as an "act of shared creation and/or shared discovery." He draws a distinction between collaboration and communication — the exchange of information, and cooperation — people working together for a common purpose without necessarily having defined that purpose. Schrage observes that the issue is not more communication but rather "it's the creation of value. Collaboration describes a process of value creation that our traditional structure of communication and teamwork can't achieve." [1]

An important component required to create new collaborative relationships will be an organization structure for the computing and library organizations that leads to a new paradigm —a campus virtual information organization.

The virtual organization has been described as a "temporary network of independent companies—suppliers, customers, even erstwhile rivals—linked by information technology to share skills, costs, and access . . . . It will have neither central office nor organization chart. It will have no hierarchy, no vertical integration. Instead . . . this new, evolving . . . model will be fluid and flexible—a group of collaborators that quickly unite to exploit a specific opportunity." [2] Computing professionals and librarians should explore this concept to determine the relevance and power of creating a virtual information organization within the university. If dynamic partnerships between professionals in computing and libraries are to flourish, the organization structure along with stated values and expectations for performance will have to be examined and redesigned to support such a relationship.

The process of creating a new organization paradigm —a virtual information organization —will benefit from individuals' understanding of existing organization principles and assumptions that underlie the current structures of libraries and computing centers.

Organization Principles

It is the organization of work and work activities that shapes relationships, communication, decision-making processes, and ultimately products and services. Collaborative work requires a particular type of environment that is in conflict with many aspects of the current organization and the principles on which it was founded.

The principles of modern organizations first emerged in the late 1700s when Adam Smith formulated the concept of the division of labor. [3] The division of labor, or segmenting of work into the smallest task, was the most prominent concept to emerge from the early industrial period. The concept rested on a desire to create efficiencies and worker productivity by having individuals perform only one task over and over again. Thus with each worker specializing in one or two simple tasks, time and effort would be more efficiently applied than if each person had to learn and perform multiple tasks and learn different tools and materials. While this approach was established primarily to increase productivity, it coincided with a view by early business owners that workers did not have the capacity or the desire to make decisions or to think about their work. Therefore, work should be at a task level and highly standardized in order to insure timely and quality production at the lowest cost.

In the early 1900s, Henry Ford combined the idea of simple and singular tasks with moving the work to the people performing the tasks—and the assembly line was born. The idea of work moving to the workers has been applied to not only automobile production but to all types of work within every conceivable type of organization. Efficiencies were achieved by moving the raw materials of work to the workers rather than the workers having to move their location. In service organizations, this not only affected the processing of paper and materials but clients (as part of the raw materials) since they had to come to the "workers" as well.

There are many examples in libraries and computing centers that reflect these early principles for organizing work. Work is segmented into functional departments to simplify complex work for the staff but not necessarily for the customer: libraries have multiple processing departments such as Acquisitions, Cataloging, Binding, Marking, Shelving while a computer center also organizes around broad functions such as administrative data processing, network support, software and equipment support, and project accounts. And the delivery of service by both computer centers and libraries require that their "customers" come to the particular facility to have questions answered, to secure certain materials or resources, and to receive instruction.

As organizations, including universities and their many departments, grew in size and scope, management was centered around functional segments or by specialists to focus on specific operations. And finally, the principle of a central staff to control activities and to coordinate various segments or functional operations became established in organizations. A hierarchical structure is now commonplace with employees and management focusing their interest, attention and communication almost exclusively within their own organizational segment. Communication and interaction among staff has evolved with a vertical orientation and lines have been drawn around working relationships with problem-solving occurring in tightly segmented units. One author describes this organization orientation as creating "functional silos." [4]

There were positive aspects of this typical organization model including consistent and predictable performance, short training periods with workers performing at the task level, and an ability to absorb turnover or to expand or contract the work force with a minimum impact on productivity and the quality of the product or service.

These principles and assumptions related to the organization of work have proved to be effective in a stable and growth environment. Beginning in the 1980s, though, the reality for organizations across the spectrum of profit and non-profit, manufacturing and service began to alter in major ways. The pace of change was greatly accelerated, economic predictability was no longer possible, competition intensified, information technology began to create new opportunities and requirements, customers became more demanding, and employees, most particularly professionals, began to demand that they have a greater say about their work and the work environment. The organization structure that served well for so many decades became increasingly dysfunctional in the turmoil of this new technological, economic, competitive and cultural environment. These realities, in addition to the vast opportunities for innovative services and products potentially available through the application of technology, suggest that now is the time to challenge primarily nineteenth century organizational principles that have shaped organizations including universities.

University computing centers and libraries, as microcosms of the university, certainly are not exempt from the many criticisms directed toward large organizations. Over the past decade these descriptions are typified by statements that organizations are suffering from bureaucratic paralysis and inflexibility, and are sluggish, inefficient and noncreative. Criticisms about large organizations also focus on their high overhead costs, in particular the expense of a large management cadre to coordinate the increasingly complex segmented organization. In addition, there is criticism that the focus of the organization is too often on activity rather than results, and that there is a lack of responsiveness or responsibility toward the client. The current organization has been described as a place where people look inward to their department and upward to their boss but no one looks outward to the client. [5]

Library and computing professionals need to assess if they —or more importantly, their "customers" —would evaluate their organizations as containing these characteristics.

Achieving Organization Effectiveness

Even as university administrators operate under considerable financial and political pressure, demands for a quality education will continue to be heard from parents, students, taxpayers, alumni and the corporate sector, which depends on a well-educated work force. Universities, through their various colleges and departments, will have to deliver a quality education despite limited financial resources.

Library and computing professionals, working together, have a unique opportunity to assist administrators and faculty in using information technology to not only create efficiencies with administrative processes but also to offer entirely new ways to organize and distribute information and to enhance education.

Some professionals, though, may resist making fundamental changes in all aspects of their work lives. Minimally, professionals will need to learn about their professional colleagues in the other organization, examine and revise as necessary their expectations regarding individual roles and responsibilities, and acquire a different set of abilities and knowledge in order to work effectively in an organization culture that is less structured, more ambiguous, and in a constant state of change.

Unless a highly fluid and flexible working environment is created, both libraries and computing centers risk a decline in their role in the university. Strangled by too few resources and unable to respond to the many and diverse expectations and demands for service and support, libraries and computing centers standing alone may indeed become the "white elephants" that some predict. A vigorous and imaginative response in this environment is required to insure that this scenario does not emerge.

One step is for the professionals to evaluate their operations to determine if the following would describe their organizations:

- fluid and flexible
- lean and efficient
- innovative and focused on continuous improvement
- responsive and timely
- results-focused rather than activity-focused
- client-centered

In the traditional hierarchical and segmented organization, common in large libraries and computing centers, the structure itself may create obstacles that limit the ability of individuals to establish these qualities in their work environment and their ability to cross the boundaries of two different organizations.

Though an effective organization is created by effective people, organization structure and work processes can facilitate or limit staff effectiveness. In considering how to improve individual effectiveness, it is necessary to assess what aspects of the organization either facilitate or create barriers for quality service. As librarians and computing professionals look not only at improving services in their individual primary areas of responsibility but at creating a truly collaborative environment for the two professional groups, the shape and culture of the organization will be important.

In *Reengineering the Organization: A Manifesto for Business Revolution,* Hammer and Champy urge that managers consider first what fundamental changes are required in the way service and products are delivered. They argue that if quality improvement is made on costly and ineffective processes, then the organization has ultimately made no real improvement.

These authors suggest that in order to achieve organization effectiveness, it is necessary to eliminate elaborate controls and to reduce layers and overhead. They suggest that managers and administrators need to consciously invent a better way of doing things—to reengineer the organization. As part of this reengineering, the requirements and role of collaborative work between librarians and computing professionals should be a central consideration.

Hammer and Champy describe reengineering the organization in the following way:

> Reengineering a company means tossing aside old systems and starting over. It involves going back to the beginning and inventing a better way of doing work. . . .it is the fundamental rethinking and radical redesign of business processes to achieve dramatic improvements in critical, contemporary measures of performance, such as cost, quality, service, and speed. [6]

The key words in this description are *fundamental, radical, dramatic,* and *processes*. And the authors stress that reengineering is not simply restructuring or downsizing, nor is it the same as reorganizing, though this may result as well as a reduction in the hierarchy. They emphasize that the problems facing organizations are not with the structure per se but with their processes. Hammer and Champy state that "the way to eliminate bureaucracy and flatten the organization is by reengineering the processes so that they are no longer fragmented." [7] Librarians and computing professionals need to ask not only themselves but their customers if there are processes — or services — they offer that result in confusion and frustration. For example, if instruction is offered to students and faculty on the use of the Internet by both professional groups how does the individual know which course to take, which is most appropriate. Fragmentation in this regard results not only in frustration but possibly damages relations with those very people that should be served by the respective professionals.

As librarians and computing professionals consider how to create a collaborative work environment, the following characteristics have been identified as key to an effective and innovative organization: [8]

- simple processes exist rather than simple jobs
- organization defined by relationships
- innovation is systematic & integral
- employees are empowered at all levels of the organization
- standardization avoided when it increases complexity
- work performed where it makes most sense (within jobs and physical location)

- central controls & checking minimized
- hybrid organization of centralized & decentralized operations exists
- client (user) is central focus of all activity

Collaborative & Team-Focused Organizations

An organization that incorporates the characteristics previously mentioned, begins to look and feel differently because individuals within the organization behave differently in accomplishing their work. Teamwork becomes central and is built on individuals grouped together to perform the various tasks related to a specific process or project. The division of labor is replaced by a division of knowledge as an organization principle. The division of knowledge focuses on bringing together individuals who have knowledge and competence for a particular process or activity. Keen views the division of knowledge as capturing "an obvious reality of work in an era of rapid change and uncertainty. Tasks are no longer predictable and experience may no longer be valuable. New inputs of knowledge are needed to define tasks and multiple skills and experience are needed to complete them."[9] In this context, the quality of individual performance rests on the quality of communication and coordination among the team members. The success of the team approach requires a commitment of all members to results and a willingness to share authority and responsibility among all members of the team, though each person brings a different set of skills and knowledge to the activities of the team. As difficult as this is to achieve within a single organization, the collaborative team environment for computing and library professionals will be built on their ability to share, across these organizational boundaries, authority and responsibility. This will not be possible unless the individuals hold respect and trust for one another and their respective talents and abilities.

Another shift in the reengineered organization is to move from strictly job training to the more developmental view of educating individuals so that they understand their work and that of their team and how it supports the overall goals of the organization. In this environment, staff are continually building their knowledge, skills and insight for future changes of the organization and those of their team. This educational approach is essential for the virtual information organization to succeed as a collaborative process.

Finally, a collaborative and team-focused organization makes it possible to involve clients in designing products and services, not only evaluating these after the fact. The involvement of the client as another partner in the collaborative effort between librarians and computing professionals is a way to ensure that all services and products do indeed add value for the client. When this environment is established, "protective" action in response to other segments of the organization or the client will not be common because it is neither valued nor rewarded. Instead it is collaboration that leads to innovation and quality service that is recognized and rewarded.

Managers in the Virtual Information Organization

As more changes occur in the organization structure and processes of the library and the computing center and as collaborative activities initiated between the professional staffs are promoted, understandably managers are uncertain regarding their role in this emerging organization. These shifts are in addition to other changes in the management environment over the past decade such as the introduction of self-managed teams, a commitment to empowering individual employees, and the distribution of decision-making throughout the organization.

New terminology as well as clear expectations regarding the role and responsibilities of managers are needed to assist individual managers, as well as those they manage, to make the transition into a team-based and collaborative organization. Managers will be key in this transition including their ability to see their own role and responsibilities differently as traditional managerial duties are reshaped for a collaborative and consultative approach rather than one of authority and control .

In this environment, the role and expectation for managers should focus on the following:
- coaching and mentoring of staff
- focusing on development of staff
- offering advice and assistance in solving problems or initiating new programs or services
- developing shared values and vision among staff
- encouraging adaptability, initiative, accountability, and teamwork
- providing resources within framework of cost and benefits assessment

- taking pride in accomplishment of others
- providing incentives so collaboration works

Some individuals will not be well suited to the new managerial construct as "team leaders" or "coaches" and this will need to be recognized and a different assignment found for these individuals. In any case, a significant commitment from the organization for the development of individual managers will be required for individuals to learn about and integrate into their philosophy and management style an understanding and respect for collaboration and team work.

Conclusion

The shape and context for organizations is being altered in potentially dramatic ways. The examination of the university organization and its many departments and units is already a reality on many campuses whether through external audits or the application of total quality management (TQM) principles. The proliferation and integration of information technology into all segments of university programs and activities suggests that computing and library professionals have an opportunity unique to their shared responsibilities to play a significant role in contributing to the shape of the university in the 21st century. They are well positioned if they work collaboratively to build on their individual and collective strengths, to provide leadership in the integration of information technology in thoughtful and innovative ways. Indeed their ability to contribute to the turbulent and rapidly changing environment will be magnified if they pursue a strength in a collaborative partnership.

As professionals explore, test, retreat and try again to find common ground on which to build the virtual information organization within the university, their focus in evaluating and designing the organization to support this effort should focus on the following:

- simplifying organization processes
- creating multi-dimension jobs
- creating a team-based and collaborative work environment
- developing individuals for job & career opportunities and preparing them for change
- shifting performance measures to results
- creating organization values & rewards based on client satisfaction

It will not be an easy task for individuals or for the organization to shift to a new culture and expectation based on collaboration. Nevertheless, it is clear that change in the current organization is urgently needed.

Schrage provides the positive context for considering the personal and organizational advantage in selecting a collaborative model for work. He states that "the best of all possible collaborative futures offers a world where people can enjoy and indulge their individuality even as they enhance and augment their communities." [10]

References

1. Michael Schrage. *Shared Minds: The New Technologies of Collaboration.* New York: Random House. 1990. p. 6.

2. John A. Byrne. "The Virtual Corporation." *Business Week* (February 8, 1993): 99.

3. Adam Smith. *An Inquiry Into the Nature and Causes of the Wealth of Nations.* ed. Edwin Cannan. Chicago: University of Chicago Press. 1979.

4. Michael Hammer and James Champy. *Reengineering the Corporation: A Manifesto for Business Revolution.* New York: Harper Collins Publisher, 1993. p. 28.

5. Ibid.

6. Ibid. 31-32.

7. Ibid. 48.

8. Carole A. Barone, "New Interpretations of Old Rules, or If the Ocean Is on the Right, You Are Headed North." *Cause/Effect.* 16 Spring '93. 11–16. Richard W. Beatty and David O. Ulrich, "Reengineering the Mature Organization." *Organizational Dynamics.* 20 Summer '91. 16-29. Peter Drucker, "The New Society of Organizations." *Harvard Business Review.* 70 Sept/Oct '92. 95-104. Peter G.W. Keen, "Redesigning the Organization Through Information Technology." *Planning Review.* 19 (May-June '91). James I. Penrod and Michael G. Dolence, "Concepts for Reengineering Higher Education." *Cause/Effect* Summer '91. 10-17. Geary A. Rummler and Alan P. Brache, "Managing the White Space." *Training.* 28 Jan '91. 55-70.

9. Keen, op. cit. 7.

10. Schrage, op. cit. 196.

LIBRARIES AND ACADEMIC COMPUTING CENTERS:
FORGING NEW RELATIONSHIPS IN A NETWORKED INFORMATION ENVIRONMENT

Stephen D. Franklin

University of California, Irvine

Introduction

Even confining oneself to relationships whose names begin with the letter "c," libraries and academic computer centers have a wide range of options and have already explored many of them. Competition, coexistence, and cooperation based on communication all come to mind.

Actually, the relationships I want to discuss are those of collaboration, as described by Michael Schrage in *Shared Minds: The New Technologies of Collaboration* (New York: Random House, 1990) and cited by Sheila Creth in her article "Creating a Virtual Information Organization: Collaborative Relationships Between Libraries and Computing Centers" (*Journal of Library Administration,* vol. 19, No 3/4, 1993, pp. 111-132), which we read in preparation for this meeting and which is reprinted in the Appendix.

In particular, I want to discuss collaboration based on shared creation and discovery and on mutually agreed upon goals. I assert that libraries and academic computing centers have mutually agreed upon goals that are based on core values of the academic enterprise in which we all work.

Whatever differences of perspective we bring to our joint endeavors are just that: differences of perspective. Our differences are what enrich our participation together. We may be different as individuals or in our organizational responsibilities, but if we understand the setting in which we operate, the commonality of our values and goals becomes much more apparent, as do the collaborative possibilities.

There are two ways in which we can look upon the genesis of our "new relationships." One is that we are being driven by necessity: "Oh, my gosh, we are downsizing, contracting, cutting the staff...." The other is that there are genuine and substantial opportunities to be seized. Some might say that the opportunities are so large as to be insurmountable. Gatherings such as this are an important step to seeing that such is not the case.

To consider these opportunities largely as technical ones invites approaching them from a position driven by a "technological imperative" to do whatever of value, however marginal or speculative, technology allows. Technology-centered approaches invite splitting the participants into what Stephen Wolff of the National Science Foundation has called "uncritical lovers and unloving critics" of technology.

Instead of such an approach, we should consider these opportunities as ones based in the social, intellectual, and cultural values we share and our universities embody. True, individually we play different roles within our institutions, but we are fortunate to be at a time when the contributions we can make to the larger academic enterprise are being brought to the fore. Whatever stereotypes have been held about computers and libraries, new perceptions and expectations about the roles and importance of each are providing us at the moment at least some measure of "center stage." Let us take advantage of that.

Our University Milieu

At the heart of what we have in common is our setting, the "university milieu," with its dual academic missions of education and research. These dual missions represent interdependent goals that usually, but not inevitably, are amenable to the collaborative relationships we seek. University libraries and academic computing centers support both missions: education, which preserves and transmits our cultural legacy, and research, which innovates, extends, and enriches this legacy.

In his superb book *Academic Tribes* (2nd ed., Urbana: University of Illinois Press, 1988), Hazard Adams offers keen insight into the university milieu in which we operate. He identifies such key aspects as "diffusion of academic authority," "diminishment of organizational allegiance," "protective coloration of eccentricity," and the fundamental antinomy that "the faculty is the university; the faculty are employees of the university." All of us who work in this milieu can appreciate and value how important it is to respect (in all senses of that word) both the social and the intellectual structures Adams so deftly characterizes.

Indeed, the new relationships we seek to forge can succeed only by drawing strength from our shared understanding of academic missions and academic tribes. A university's single, most valued asset is its faculty. We can help leverage the value of this asset by recognizing and assisting well-established faculty and institutional strategies in these ways: foster autonomy and initiative, cultivate collaboration, promote intramural ties, facilitate discipline-based ties, and balance competing demands.

University libraries and academic computing centers can also play critical facilitative and operational roles in establishing and maintaining participation of faculty in the world-wide academic community, with its emphasis on long-range, long-term connections, interconnections and interdependencies.

Our Machines

Libraries and computing centers are both the product of machines. A 1992 internationally produced public television series bore the title "The Machine That Changed The World." It was about computers. While this may seem an overstatement or a somewhat premature claim for computers, there can be no such qualms about so characterizing the printing press. A conclusive discussion of the parallels between the computer-mediated communications (including both computers and electronic networks) and the printing press is definitely both premature and much beyond the scope of this talk. But I most strongly recommend very close reading of Elizabeth Eisenstein's *The Printing Revolution in Early Modern Europe* (Cambridge: Cambridge University Press, 1983; paperback, 1993), a very accessible, illustrated abridgement of her two-volume *The Printing Press as an Agent of Change: Communications and Cultural Transformations in Early Modern Europe* (Cambridge: Cambridge University Press, 1979). It is impossible to read either without seeing deep and pervasive parallels between the developments she presents and our current situation with computers and networking.

Such parallels also manifest themselves in university libraries and academic computing centers. Typically, each has substantial operational responsibilities for creating and maintaining stable environments and infrastructure. Typically, each also works with key innovators in developing capabilities and in broadening availability and impact. Also, each finds that its continued relevance, contributions, and importance are open to (continuing) reexamination.

I have said "typically," but the truth is that there is significantly greater variation in academic computing centers than in university libraries. This is to be expected, as the "machine" around which the library has flourished goes back some 500 years more than the cornerstone of the computing center. As such, a few words about the academic computing milieu is not out of place. "Academic" puts the focus squarely on computing as an immediate part of education and research, quite different from the necessary administrative work computers also perform. "Computing" must include electronic network connectivity. Staggering heterogeneity and interconnectivity are essential characteristics of both the academic enterprise and any significant use of "computing" within that enterprise. Faculty autonomy, diverse disciplinary demands, and interinstitutional (human) connections make networking heterogenous systems imperative.

The truth is that just as telephone handsets are of value only insofar as they access a telephone network and even then only to the extent that they provide communications between individuals (or such agents as fax machines), similarly the real value of "computer networks" is in their ability to interconnect people and systems; to lessen, or even eliminate, the impact of spatial separation and temporal shifts, in facilitating resource and information sharing, and in promoting and sustaining interpersonal contacts. "Computer-mediated communication" may be a cumbersome phrase, but it will have to do until more felicitous wording evolves over time. "Printer-mediated communications" would be equally cumbersome if we didn't have alternate wording honed by centuries of use.

The litany of networked-based computer services and functionality has been rehearsed in too many other forums to justify anything more than a cursory list here: remote system access/login, remote peripheral services, file transfer, electronic mail, mailing lists, listservers, electronic bulletin boards, newsgroups, networked/distributed file systems, wide area information servers, and so forth. The truth is that any number of widely available books now do an excellent job of describing the rivers of "information" and a moderately adequate job of offering hope of finding a cup with which one can drink from the torrent.

On the other hand, over 500 years of coping with the printing presses' output have not made it an easy task for any but the well trained, backed by tools fashioned over an equal period of time, to navigate the seas of printed matter. Consider how much of our educational system is constructed to develop such facility. "Computer people" need not yet apologize to "printing press people" for difficulties navigating electronic oceans.

The Internet

In their pioneering book *The Internet Companion: A Beginner's Guide to Global Networking* (Addison-Wesley, 1992), Tracy LaQuey and Jeanne Ryer write, "The Internet is a loose amalgam of thousands of computer networks reaching millions of people all over the world."

More precise statements are available (and guaranteed to be obsolete before one can proofread them), but few carry the essential character of "The Net" any better.

A conservative estimate of network growth is to say that by most measures it at least doubles every year. One of the few things seeming to grow as quickly is the proliferation of specialized terminology. Fortunately, network and jargon growth has been matched by a hoard of enterprising individuals and companies who now provide a broad and varied range of publications (print and electronic) and services to help us keep pace with these changes.

Rather than plunge into the jargon jungle and symbol soup in which technical conversations thrive, let us simply recognize that specialized terminology has proved a necessary tool in virtually every area of human endeavor. The increasingly common appearance of a particular technology's jargon is both an indication and a facilitation of the increasing importance and deployment of that technology.

We are fortunate in the number and range of authors and articles making the technology and its underlying concepts familiar to a broad audience. Indeed, some of the principal innovators have provided remarkably good descriptions of their work (cf. "The World-Wide Web," T. Berners-Lee, R. Cailliau, A. Luotonen, H.F. Nielson, and A. Secret, *Communications of the Association for Computing Machinery,* August 1994, v. 37, No. 8, pp. 76-82).

Would that Gutenberg and Schoeffer had been so capable and inclined!

Balancing Innovation and Stability

Both university libraries and academic computing centers have substantial operational responsibilities that require the overwhelming portion of their resources and attention. While partnership in these activities may have some benefits, the most fertile ground for collaboration and the areas where there is the most need for partnership both involve exploring possibilities that did not exist even a few years ago.

A central challenge to each organization in forging new relationships is how to balance innovation and stability, especially where the latter includes substantial and critical operational responsibilities that are outside the collaborative scope. That the collaboration focuses on a limited portion of each organization's scope can be an advantage if (and only if) there is broad recognition that the collaborative effort can contribute to each organization's larger scope of activities in the not-so-distant future. It is important that the collaboration help all parties "pick low-hanging fruit" rather than build ladder segments that reach toward tantalizing, distant attractions.

Even without the challenges and opportunities of collaboration, balancing change and continuity is no easy matter in general and is particularly "interesting" (as in the folk curse "May you live in interesting times") with computers and networking these days. Change is necessary but generates both personal and institutional stress and hysteresis.

> "It is never a good time to buy a new system."

> "It is always a good time to buy a new system."

Both are true.

"Backward compatibility" conveys a similar, paradoxically true double meaning. One doesn't want to sacrifice previous work, but progress is retarded by excessive adherence to previous efforts that were based on a perspective that has been superseded by the very success of these efforts. One can move a rowboat by casting the anchor in the direction one wants to go and pulling on the line after the anchor has settled. But one must lift the anchor off the bottom before the boat passes over it lest the pull on the line become a retarding or even regressive force.

Faculty provide an additional dimension to this situation because they are used to being on the cutting edge in their own disciplines. Some will want to stay toward the leading (bleeding) edge with technology. Some will stay with what they first or already learned until they absolutely have to change (if ever). Between these extremes are those who wait until the immediate benefits to their work outweigh the effort of such a change.

Faculty and students need to maintain their academic foci even as they adjust to changes in the tools and resources available to them. While personal experience is invaluable and faculty especially draw on it, its limitations are proverbial: "Experience runs a fine school, but the tuition is most dear." That "tuition" is paid in time, energy, and intelligence. An abiding and central strength of the professional staff of both university libraries and academic computing centers is the ability to work with faculty and students in making the best use of this "tuition." Ultimately, it is this strength that is at the heart of our collaboration.

Postscript

Many people, myself included, feel that computer/network electronic access to information represents an innovation comparable to the introduction of the movable-type printing press. We see the World-Wide Web as an exciting, if still primitive, technological realization of the type of organization of information and even knowledge that heretofore was realized in footnotes, references, and the minds of individuals. It begins to realize the "associative indices" and "memex" of Vannevar Bush's landmark article of half a century ago, "As We May Think" (*Atlantic Monthly,* vol. 176, no. 1, July 1945, pp. 101-108).

At the same time, one wonders what type of world this new technology will help create. As an encouragement to look to the past as one considers the future, I offer the following "postscript."

A curiously coincidental collection of connections of words leads from "PostScript" as the (trademarked) name of a page-description language from Adobe, a company that has recently purchased a company named "Aldus," maker of "Aldus Pagemaker." But there was an historic Aldus and his name was not "Pagemaker," although pagemaker/publisher he was. Aldo Manzio (1450?-1515), known as Aldus Manutius, was a pivotal and fascinating figure in the early years of scholarly publishing. In the 1508 edition of his *Adages,*

Erasmus writes

> Once, this [restoration of learning] was the task of princes
> and it was the greatest glory of Ptolemy.... But his library
> was contained between the narrow walls of its own house,
> and Aldus is building up a library which has no other lim-
> its than the world itself.
>
> M.M. Phillips, "Adages" of Erasmus, Cambridge
University Press, 1964, pp. 180-181.

"The library without walls," or at least a library as large as the world
itself, has an honorable and ancient pedigree. Ours is the opportunity to collaborate on the fuller realization of this vision, giving it a
substance and meaning that only personal network-based computing has made possible.

Upbeat, technophilic readers can stop here.

A more balanced view, acknowledging the somber side of the situation is suggested in the closing words of Martin Lowry's *The World
of Aldus Manutius* (Cornell University Press, 1979):

> But as the manuscript disappeared, a great part of Aldus'
> world disappeared with it.... If Aldus died a melancholy
> man, it was not without reason: for he had played a great
> part in destroying the world that had created him, and he
> could not yet foresee the veneration in which he would
> be held by the new world that he was calling into being.

Whichever view one prefers, "printing press people" and "computer
people" share more than they hold separately.

ENHANCING USER SERVICES THROUGH COLLABORATION AT RICE UNIVERSITY

Kay Flowers and Andrea Martin
Rice University

Cooperation between the library and the computer center at Rice University has had its ups and downs for thirty years. Cooperation was down in the summer of 1985 when the computing center proposed running the library's then new NOTIS system on the existing campus mainframe, and the library declined and purchased its own minicomputer. Yet by the summer of 1993, we had created a new department, User Services, made up of the personnel in several public service areas of the library as well as the public service areas of the computer center. Members of this staff group, although located in different campus buildings, are working to address information services for the Rice University community. This article discusses some of the milestones along the path from a position of no cooperation to a combined user-centered service organization, including collaborative outgrowths of this new structure.

Environment

Rice University is a small, private research university founded in 1912. It has a strong engineering and science program. Fondren Library has 1.5 million volumes with a staff of around 120. We face the usual budget and space concerns. Computing supports over 6,000 users with around eighty staff. Since Rice was one of the original Apple Consortium schools, we have a large installed base of Macintosh computers. We also have a wide deployment of Unix workstations in Engineering and Science, and are completing a campus-wide wiring project.

Until recent reorganizations, the information systems support structure at Rice emphasized turf. We had an entrenched computing organization built around mainframe computing that had existed for thirty years. The library had its own systems group and ran its own machine, as did other academic and administrative departments on campus. The philosophy of "every department as its own kingdom" prevailed. But times change.

Early collaborative efforts

In 1984, a report produced by the Self-Study Committee on Computing contained several recommendations for changes in the way computing services were provided to the campus. In 1986, as a result of one of these recommendations, Rice hired a "computing czar," an associate provost responsible for all computing on campus. He, in turn, began to implement some of the other recommendations of the self-study, including a central computing information service and an expansion of computing resources to other locales, including the library. Since he recognized the potential for library involvement in several of these projects, he encouraged joint committees for planning and implementation. These projects were the first major steps in collaboration.

Library in the computing center

The self-study committee recommended a computing information service with one-stop shopping for those interested in purchasing machines. This idea was expanded to include common reference tools used by computing staff. The final product combined manuals, reserve copies of software, and journals with reference service to create a library for campus computing users and staff. As a new venture, the Computing Reference Area (CRA) required the services of a staff librarian to create the facility and manage the collection. In developing the partnership, the library contributed a librarian position and cataloging services, and computing provided funds and materials for the collection.

This project had several outcomes. First, librarians gained experience working in a new setting. The systems environment in the computing center emphasized Macintosh and Unix, while the library was installing x86 machines for DOS and Windows-based software. While there were no major "culture collisions," staff noticed and discussed differences. The most obvious of these was salary. The salary differential between librarians and technologists became more salient to the librarians, particularly when hiring the librarian to manage the facility. While everyone agreed that this person could be a beginning librarian, or one with limited experience who could grow with the job, the computer center suggested the title "manager" for this position and suggested a salary that was $7,000 more than the then-current salary for an entry level librarian. In addition, having the librarian report in two areas created some management challenges, but communication between the two groups increased.

Computing lab in the library

Another self-study recommendation to extend computing led to the creation of a computing lab in the library. Known as the Center for Scholarship and Information (CSI), this lab was used to enhance the teaching of English through the use of computers. Planned at the same time as the CRA, the CSI also included video and software in an area containing viewing facilities as well as computers arranged in a classroom configuration, thus encouraging the use of technology in the classroom. Creating the CSI involved a collaboration of faculty, librarians, and computing staff.

The project met with mixed results. As an electronic classroom, the facility was used actively by English and biology classes. As an experiment with technology, it experienced problems with limited space, inadequate funding, and staff turnover. Another problem was that, originally, the project was governed by a large committee of faculty, librarians, and computing professionals as well as the staff of the facility. Each group had different concerns and goals: faculty members were concerned with teaching in the classroom, librarians were concerned with collection and staffing, and the computing professionals were concerned with equipment and funding. Progress was hindered by the diffusion of responsibility and conflicts in interests. Eventually, the full committee ceased to meet, with day-to-day operations handled by the librarian with oversight for CSI and funding questions handled by computing.

Campus-wide information system

Unlike the previous two collaborations developed as part of a formal planning process, the Rice campus-wide information system (CWIS) project was born out of chaos. Both librarians and computing professionals knew about developments in this area, but were unable to pull together enough resources to make the vision a reality. Finally, the assistant director of computing services and the assistant university librarian for automated services convened a group that developed a common vision of providing electronic information to the campus. From this initial meeting, RiceInfo was born.

RiceInfo, a Gopher-based CWIS formally launched in the spring of 1993, has proved to be a powerful tool in the University. It provides access to a wide range of national and international databases mounted at other institutions in both the public and private sector and covering a broad range of disciplines. Some of RiceInfo's sources include LIBRIS, the library's online catalog; a database of research and grant opportunities maintained by our Office of Sponsored Research; the University's course catalog; and the Library of Congress catalog. RiceInfo has been cited in several recent publications as one of the places to surf the Internet.[1]

With the RiceInfo project, both groups brought strength to the table: librarians in information organization and creation, and computing staff with software and hardware support. Librarians have assumed roles in verifying information in Gopher trees, locating new information, and suggesting tree organization. Computing professionals maintain all the software and hardware and load data. We share the task of contacting volunteers to be data maintainers. All of us have had uneven levels of cooperation in working with these information providers, but we have built a resource that is nationally recognized.

Virtual library

Soon after the RiceInfo effort got under way, some librarians were asked to develop a plan for creatively dealing with electronic resources. They started work on a position paper identifying strategies to pursue for different formats of electronic information: software to be reviewed, hardware needed, and data to purchase or lease. As they worked they found they needed more expertise, and the original committee grew to include members of the computing center staff. The "Virtual Fondren" project, as this effort was called, identified desired tools and developed plans for their purchase. RiceInfo was selected as the best means for delivery of the Virtual Fondren electronic information, and resources were acquired as the first step in extending electronic access to traditional library information.

As a result of this project, RiceInfo now includes some critical informational resources provided through purchase and subscription. Some of these resources are databases mounted using the WAIS software and searchable with keywords: Current Contents, a database of scientific journals and publications; the Modern Language Association Bibliography, a database of journals and books covering language, literature, and linguistics; and the Expanded Academic Index, an index of general periodicals in many areas. Other resources are provided remotely through subscriptions to services: CARL Uncover, a database of tables of contents of journals and a related document delivery service; OCLC FirstSearch, including access to the WorldCat database and others; and RLG's Citadel service, including the Avery Index to architectural information.

Collaborations leading to change

By 1989, the original associate provost in charge of computing had become a vice president in charge of information systems, including the library, thus formalizing some of the ongoing collaboration. The first person to fill this job left in 1991 and was replaced by a man with a vision for technology in the classroom. As this vision was explored, more efforts at collaboration were undertaken with an emphasis on teaching and learning. Thus the stage was set for change.

Electronic Studio project

In 1990, the Computer Planning Board of the University envisioned a new educational environment for the University—the Electronic Studio—in which to prepare students for the world of the future. This vision involved an integration of information technology in the classroom and at the desktop. In 1992, with the hiring of the new information systems vice president, an intensive effort began to realize this vision on the campus.

Originally compared to an architect's studio, the Electronic Studio is an environment for collaborative work with all necessary tools easily available. But unlike other types of studios, the Electronic Studio is not bound to a single place. The stage, models, and props of the Electronic Studio are built from complex webs of text, graphics, video, and audio. The productions organize these elements in novel ways to serve the needs of students and teachers from different disciplines. Written theories are transformed into demonstrations, and models into simulations. Audio annotations can be heard, and digitized video for demonstrations can be an integral part of collaborative work among teachers, students, and librarians. The Electronic Studio has provided the paradigm for most recent collaborations, for everyone is involved in providing the technology and information to enhance learning and research.

Curriculum development

By 1993, the Electronic Studio project had begun to focus on creating prototypes for curriculum development. These prototypes involved librarians and technologists working to find appropriate solutions for faculty. Librarians assisted in locating information in all formats to be incorporated into the curriculum, while computing professionals assisted in working with the software available to provide the faculty member with the correct tools for presenting material. Student assistants provided scanning and documentation support. Each course had a leader, either a librarian or a computing professional, working with the faculty member and several students to develop the course. Survey courses in the history of art and architecture gained detailed image study guides, a national security policy course reviewed the conduct of the Persian Gulf War, and an introductory biosciences class recorded lab data online.

The Electronic Studio curriculum projects provided a lab for experimenting with collaboration among librarians, computing center staff, and faculty. Each project also offered valuable insights into the possible dynamics of electronic studios. While each project required different expertise, all emphasized the collaborative nature of learning.

Table 1 (see next page) lists courses that were deployed in the 93-94 academic year. The 94-95 academic year will see the deployment of additional courses as well as an electronic reserve system.

One aspect of these projects that is evident from the table is the wide variety of tools used in developing courses. The Virtual Notebook System, VNS, is collaborative client/server software based on the metaphor of a medical researcher's notebook.[2] Users record information on pages that can be shared with other members of the lab or class, thus encouraging collaboration over time and distance. Pages can include text, images, and graphics, and links to other applications, and notebooks of pages can be secured. Mosaic, a World-Wide Web client, also integrates text and images as well as video and audio in its presentation of information. It offers wide access, but less security. AutoCad is familiar to most as a drafting tool, and Wavefront and xanim are used to animate and display drawings and renderings. More common software, such as newsreaders, can be used in the classroom to provide insight into current events, as was demonstrated in the course on the Gulf War.

Table 1: Projects deployed during the 1993-94 academic year

Course	Name	Tools Used
Poli 378	American National Security Policy	Virtual Notebook System (VNS), Mosaic
Hist 269	U.S.–Latin American Relations	VNS, Mosaic, newsreaders
Huma 102	Humanities Foundation	VNS
Hart 412	Michelangelo	VNS
Hart 205	Art History: Introduction	VNS, Mosaic
Arch 346	History of Modern Architecture	VNS
Arch 440/640	Advanced Computer Modeling	VNS, Wavefront, AutoCad, xanim
Arch 667	The Architecture of LeCorbusier	VNS, student authoring
Hart 345	Renaissance & Baroque Architecture	VNS
Bios 211	Introduction to BioSciences	Basic
Bios 213	Introduction to BioSciences	MacVNS, QuickTime, Basic
Bios 317	Introduction to BioSciences	MacVNS, QuickTime, Basic
Bios 418	Molecular Biophysics	VNS, imaging software
Math 211	Differential Equations	VNS

The scope of the Electronic Studio projects provided the impetus to develop the necessary infrastructure for future efforts of this kind. Service and support are critical to this infrastructure. With the expansion of computing in the classroom, the numbers and types of users expanded with the types of software supported, thus straining the service organization that was in place at the computing center. In addition, the types of questions asked broadened. Now, users of Electronic Studio materials could ask questions about the software, the hardware, or the information itself. As these projects began, the staff of the computing center was not in a position to answer these types of questions that more traditionally fell in the library's area. Yet, the question remained of how to provide quick, straightforward service for a group of users that would not have straightforward questions.

Organizational change

The installation of network wiring across the campus, the increasing number of electronic library resources, the deployment of higher-end workstations in the labs, the prototype Electronic Studio curriculum projects with their wide array of software, and the migration to a new library system—all these projects served as catalysts for change. As a result of the increasing numbers of computing users, particularly whole classes of users, we were compelled to improve user services while being constrained by a freeze on staff growth. These constraints led to the creation, in the summer of 1993, of a new organization focused on users.

Figure 1 shows the overall divisional perspective of the restructured Information Systems organization, with five major areas:

- Administrative Computing—financial system, student information system
- Networking Services—VM and DEC support, networking
- Computing Services —user services, Unix systems support, business services
- Fondren Library
- Administration and Leadership—vice president, directors of each group

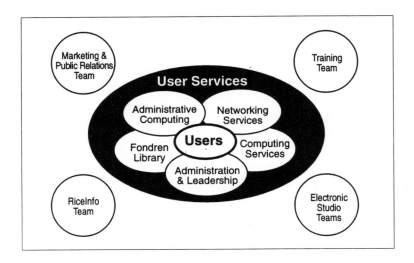

Figure 1: Information Systems Division view

We also had projects that crossed organizational boundaries. For example, the marketing and public relations team involved publications and consulting staff from computing with PR staff in the library. The training team combined training staff from the library with training staff from computing. The RiceInfo team combined reference librarians, systems programmers from Networking Services, and consulting staff. And the Electronic Studio team combined staff from all over the organization—networking staff, Unix systems administrators, divisional consultants, librarians, and grant-funded programmers.

Within the new organizational model, users are the central focus, and User Services is the thread that binds the entire division. The new User Services group combines consultants, trainers, technical writers, and LAN specialists from computing with librarians from the reference and government publications areas. At the same time, we maintained a project team focus that allows us to address new tasks rapidly; some of the cross-functional project teams are shown in separate bubbles in the figure.

The library perspective is shown in Figure 2 (see next page). The library is organized into:

- Technical Services—cataloging, database management, acquisitions

- Special Services—satellite collections, Woodson research center, community services

- Library IT—integrated library system, microcomputer support

- User Services—reference, government publications, A/V services, training, publications, lab services

- Administration and Leadership—librarian, heads of the other groups, some staff

The library also participates in the project groups described above and shown as bubbles in the figure. Again, users are the focus of the organization, with the various departments supporting them. User Services is in the area usually occupied by public services.

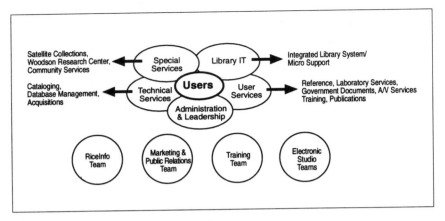

Figure 2: IS Division/Fondren Library view

Within User Services (see Figure 3 for this view), staff are divided into teams managed by team leaders or managers, depending on the size of the group. Groups include Consulting Support, Reference, and Government Publications and Special Services. Teams include LAN support, divisional consulting representatives, the training team, and the publications team as well as other special project teams. The team and group leaders meet weekly with the assistant director of computing services, who in turn reports to a board consisting of the Information Systems group directors. As the figure illustrates, users are still the central focus.

With our new organization, the focus is on serving customers. Customers have one interface to the organization, which implies that the rest of the organization must provide adequate backroom support. In the new group, librarians and computing professionals are working side by side as part of the same team. As the reference paradigm expands, computing consultants are learning about reference, and librarians are learning about computer consulting. Our vision for the future is a help/reference desk that is staffed by librarians and computer consultants.[3]

In implementing the new structure, we have experienced some challenges, primarily with differences in culture and tool sets. The culture of the library was passive-aggressive, whereas some computing staff bordered on aggressive-abrasive. This difference was very evident in project team meetings that would be dominated by computing staff opinions. Library staff often would remain quiet during meetings, allowing moderators to believe that consensus had been

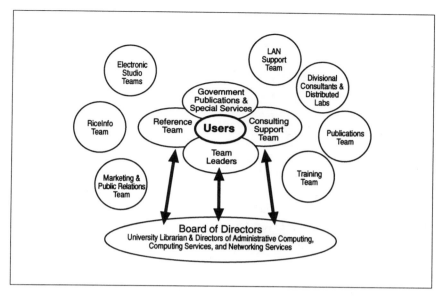

Figure 3: IS Division/User Services view

reached, but later would complain to their peers rather than discuss problems with the project group or management. Through weekly team-leader meetings, combined staff projects, combined social functions, and joint training sessions, we have begun to overcome some of these differences. By working together, staff from both computing and the library have come to appreciate their skill and knowledge differences, and create a relationship of trust and respect for their colleagues.

In the case of tool sets, librarians favored PCs while computing staff used Unix. With some additional funding, workstations and training were provided for the librarians, who now compete for access to them.

Due to an upper management constraint, we did not have adequate time to build consensus for the new organization. The initial staff meetings were difficult, with both groups claiming, "They're taking over." Librarians were anxious about answering software questions, and computing professionals were concerned that they would work the reference desk. However, through working together on projects, the staff have begun to create long-term relationships that will help the organization focus on future endeavors.

Collaborations in progress

Since the reorganization, we have continued to embark on success-ful collaborations. Two examples, in progress, are the campus wir-ing project and the Information Arcade.[4]

Year of the Network

In the summer of 1993, we began a project to extend the campus network to every academic and administrative office on the cam-pus. Affectionately called "Year of the Network," the project involved library and computing staff from its inception. Both staffs share re-sponsibility for delivering information sessions and training. The combination of the librarians' faculty ties with the technical depth of computing staff have led to positive experiences for many new customers. The project has been a lot of work—phase 1 involved 795 new ports in fifty-one departments. However, the experiences have led to increased interaction with our customers.

Information Arcade

The Information Arcade was proposed in the fall of 1993 as a show-case learning center in the library. Phase 1 will include small-group, computer-facilitated interaction spaces, areas for individual infor-mation exploration, an electronic text center, a curriculum develop-ment center, and an electronic classroom. When space for expan-sion becomes available in a few years, the concept will be expanded to include a combined reference/help desk.

While this project has involved computing and library staff from its inception, several problems occurred. A multi-thread design pro-cess had several groups working in parallel without appropriate communication. We encountered political resistance to the first and later designs. Fondren Library was remodeled in 1989, but no space was added, and one area was remodeled for another department. Therefore, physical space in the library is a precious commodity, and several groups fought for their turf. We also had a re-emergence of the "computing is taking over the library" fear from staff and fac-ulty. Most of these problems were overcome by expanding the plan-ning committee to achieve a greater consensus.

When the facility is completed in the fall of 1994, the library will become a center for information technology on the campus. Stu-dents will have additional workspaces, and faculty will have access to new services. We will also have a production center for future Electronic Studio curriculum projects.

Conclusion

Historically, the library has focused on the acquisition, organization, preservation, access to, and automation of information. Computing has traditionally provided machine cycles and tools, emphasizing technology with information provision as a by-product. The collaborations we have described build on these strengths, while providing the opportunity for growth for both groups and the development of new skills.

Our new service model identifies information technology as the pillar of our operation, with the library and computing services as strategic partners. Given diminishing resources, we do not have time for turf wars. The kinds of changes that we are encountering demand a systematic, not incremental, response.

Our experiences have led us to conclude that in creating collaborative projects, it is important to recognize that not everything works the first time, and some things may never work. However, given time to build relationships and foster communication, the kinds of collaborations that we have described are possible, and the potential gain in creativity substantial. In the present economic realities of higher education, such projects offer one way to make the best use of staff resources.

References:

1. "Netsurf," *Wired*, December 1993, p. 126; and Loss Pequeño Glazier, "Internet Resources for English and American Literature," *C&RL News*, July/August 1994, p. 421.

2. G. Anthony Gorry, Kevin B. Long, Andrew M. Burger, Cynthia P. Jung, and Barry D. Meyer, "The Virtual Notebook System: An Architecture for Collaborative Work," *Journal of Organizational Computing* 1 (1991): 233-250.

3. Additional information on the new organization is available in a recent publication by Kevin Brook Long and Beth J. Shapiro, "On Paths that Have Converged: Libraries and Computing Centers," *Library Issues* 14 (July 1994): 1-4.

4. The Information Arcade name (trademark application pending) and concept originated at the University of Iowas Libraries in 1992.

Appendix 1

Program Agenda of the Institute

BUILDING PARTNERSHIPS: LIBRARY AND COMPUTING PROFESSIONALS

Library Solutions Institute #3
co-sponsored with CICNet, Inc.
May 12-14, 1994
Big-10 Conference Center, Chicago, Illinois

THURSDAY		
7:00pm-7:30pm	Registration	*Location: Press Room*
7:30-10:00pm	Welcome	Anne Lipow, Mike Staman, Sheila Creth
	Keynote address	Sara Kiesler
		Collaborative Relationships: New Ways of Working Together in the Networked Environment
	Reception follows	Desserts and beverages
		Meet your "Off-Campus Partners"

FRIDAY		
7:30-8:30am	Breakfast with Off-Campus Partners	
8:15am	Announcements	
	CONTEXTS	
8:40-10:40	Stephen Franklin	Developments in the networked information environment: a fertile ground for forging new relationships
	NEW MODELS: Creating a Vision	
	Small Groups Task No. 1: Designing a future together	
10:40-11:00	Break	
11:00-noon	**Plenary Session**	
	Reports from small groups and discussion	
	What you say about your roles: Summary of "Quick-Task" contributions	
12:00-1:10	Lunch with Off-Campus Partners (optional)	
1:00pm	Announcements	
1:15	**CONTEXTS: Case Studies**	
	Andrea Martin & Kay Flowers	Collaboration at Rice University
	Selected participants	Reports about collaboration-in-progress
2:30	Break	
	CONTEXTS	
3:00-3:45	Sheila Creth	Organizational changes required to achieve collaboration
	NEW MODELS: Bringing the Vision Closer	
3:45-5:15	Small Groups Task No. 2: Inventing new organizational models	
5:15	Plenary Session: Review of progress on organizational models	
5:30	Adjourn	
	[Evening: Small groups complete Task No. 2, if not done by 5:30]	

over--▶

SATURDAY 7:30-8:30am 8:15	Breakfast [Small groups complete Task No. 2, if not yet done] Announcements
8:40-9:30	New Organizational Models: Reports from small groups
9:30-10:45am	**NEW MODELS: GETTING THERE** Soapboxes: **HOT Issues: Analysis and Critique** Explanation of soapbox sessions Anne Lipow Organizational Models.............................Host: Sheila Creth Technology and Collaboration................Host: Steve Franklin Training and Development.......................Host: Anne Lipow Rice University Collaboration................Host: Andrea Martin/Kay Flowers OTHER Partnerships..............................Host: Anita Lowry YOUR Topic/Model.................................Host: Volunteers welcome! *Break refreshments will be available at buffet table throughout this session.*
10:45-noon	Plenary Session Task No. 3: Building Bridges to Get Where We Want to Go
noon-1:15	Lunch with Off-Campus AND Home Partners (optional)
1:15-2:25	**HOME PARTNERS Task No. 4: Practical Next Steps: What Will You Do on Monday?**
2:30-3:30	**Plenary Session:** **Next-Steps Exchange** **and** **TALKBACK:** Tying loose ends, program evaluation, and suggested next steps for Institute
3:30	Adjourn

APPENDIX 2

This section contains descriptions by participants of collaborative projects that were already underway on their campuses at the time of the Institute.

THE KNOXVILLE LIBRARY/COMPUTER CENTER PARTNERSHIP
Gayle S. Baker, University of Tennessee

A LEGACY OF PARTNERSHIP:
THE UNIVERSITY OF AKRON'S LIBRARIES AND COMPUTER CENTER
Onadell Bly and Rick Wiggins, University of Akron

AREAS OF COOPERATION BETWEEN THE LIBRARY AND COMPUTING
Terri Fishel and Peg Shultz, Macalester College

BUILDING A TEAM-BASED, INTEGRATED
INFORMATION SERVICES ORGANIZATION
Joy Hughes and Charlene Grass, Oregon State University

CONSOLIDATION, CENTRALIZATION, CONNECTIONS,
AND COOPERATION AT INDIANA STATE UNIVERSITY
*Ron G. Martin, H. Scott Davis, M.K. Chatterji, and Roseann Toulson
Indiana State University*

AN OPPORTUNITY: COOPERATION BETWEEN THE LIBRARY
AND COMPUTER SERVICES
James L. Mullins, Indiana University South Bend

DOCUMENTS TO THE PEOPLE: A COLLABORATIVE APPROACH
James Ostlund and Maureen Gleason, University of Notre Dame

LIBRARY EXPLORER: INFORMATION SKILLS, STRATEGIES, AND SOURCES
Janice Simmons-Welburn and Marsha Forys, University of Iowa

UCI LIBRARIES INTERNET INFORMATION ACCESS VIA WORLD-WIDE WEB
Lorelei Tanji, University of California, Irvine

THE KNOXVILLE LIBRARY / COMPUTER CENTER PARTNERSHIP

Gayle S. Baker
Electronic Services Coordinator, University of Tennessee
baker@utklib.lib.utk.edu

In 1991, the Dean of the University of Tennessee, Knoxville (UTK) Libraries and the Director of the University of Tennessee Computing Center (UTCC) formed a group called the Joint Concerns Committee to discuss common issues and converging interests. The group has been meeting on a monthly basis. The UTK Libraries are represented by staff from the following departments: Systems, Electronic Services, Reference, and Acquisitions, while the UTCC has members from User Services, Network Hardware Engineering, and the VAX Systems Group. Initial discussions centered on the need for a campus-wide information system (CWIS), with both parties ending up developing their own applications using different software. During the last year, discussions have focused on problems with electronic mail addressing, security, increasing the size of the modem pool, campus networking plans, and the need for an authorization system. The Joint Concerns Committee has been effective, not only for problem solving but also for understanding the common ground between the two groups. In the final analysis, the Committee came to the conclusion that the UTK Libraries and the UTCC must work together to provide information services in a networked environment.

In the summer of 1994, the Joint Concerns Committee formed an ad hoc Instructional Services Task Force to study ways in which the UTCC and the UTK Libraries could work together with respect to instruction. Members of both groups were represented. The task force developed the following goals:

Short Term

- Shared schedule of open instructional sessions provided by UTCC and UTK Libraries. This should be in place for the 1995 spring term.

- Development of more joint publications.

- Development of joint orientation program for new faculty and students.

- Orientation for UTK Libraries staff to what UTCC offers, and vice versa.

- Reading and discussion of UTCC Computing Conduct Code and Library Bill of Rights to broaden understanding of philosophical underpinnings and missions—what we have in common, where we differ.

Medium Term (Requires more joint planning and in-depth work.)

- Development of joint intensive training courses. UTCC already has some of these in place. It would be useful to pull in subject expertise from the library to add a new facet to these courses.

Long Term (Requires much more substantial commitment and work from both groups.)

- University Information Fair.

- Credit courses (also in conjunction with the School of Information Sciences).

- Short courses.

The UTCC and the UTK Libraries also collaborated on the publication "University Libraries/Computing Center: Resources." First appearing in the summer of 1993, this publication was a direct result of discussions initiated in the UTCC/UTK Libraries Joint Concerns Committee. The format is an eight-page tabloid with information on the various information resources, including photographs, maps, and phone numbers, as well as some general descriptions of resources and services. Another issue was published in the fall of 1994 and was aimed at new students and new faculty members.

With the demand for more computing facilities across campus, the UTK Libraries and the UTCC worked together to establish a new microcomputer laboratory on the ground floor of the John C. Hodges Library in 1993. The facility is managed by UTCC.

LIS 590, "Communications and Information Resources on the Internet," has been a very popular course in the School of Information Sciences. Tamara Miller, Head of Systems of the UTK Libraries, and Margaret Mason, User Services Consultant from UTCC, designed the course and taught it as a team for the past several semesters. Students, faculty, and staff from across the campus have taken this course.

The OLIS (Online Library Information System) Task Force was formed in 1993 to develop the RFI and RFP for a new information system for the library. Three persons from the university computing community are members. They are from Network Hardware Engineering, the Office of Academic Computing, and Administrative Information Systems. As of this writing, the task force is still active.

A Legacy of Partnership:

The University of Akron's Libraries and Computer Center

Onadell Bly
Systems Librarian, Bierce Library
rlojb@dax.cc.uakron.edu

Rick Wiggins
Network Project Leader, Computer Center
rickwiggins@uakron.edu

University of Akron

As far back as 1970, the University of Akron's libraries and Computer Center have shared a remarkable history of "working together." From an Acquisitions batch system supported by the Computer Center to the first online catalog installed in the library in 1984 to the present day, the libraries and Computer Center have had an ever-growing partnership. The OhioLINK project, first proposed by the Ohio Board of Regents in the late 1980s, has cemented that relationship and further demonstrated the ability of two diverse units to work together for the good of the entire campus and state.

Before OhioLINK can be discussed, a brief description of the development of academic networking in Ohio is needed. The Ohio Academic Resources Network (OARnet) has been a provider of Internet services in Ohio since 1987. A wide spectrum of Internet services ranging from dial-up to T1 (1.5Mbps) leased-line connections are offered through OARnet. Clients come from a broad base—from small businesses to Fortune 500 corporations. Currently, OARnet has clients in seven states; 75% are commercial clients and 25% are academic institutions and nonprofit organizations. OhioLINK utilizes OARnet to provide network connectivity to all of the participating institutions.

Network connectivity for the University's microcomputer labs, faculty members' offices, and administrative offices is provided via Zippy's Internet Protocol Network (ZIPnet). This is a high-speed data network available across campus that has a connection to OARnet, the statewide network. Primary access to OhioLINK is from workstations utilizing ZIPnet. Dial-in access to ZIPnet is available and provides VT100 and IBM 3270 emulation for access to university computer services. Development of Point-to-Point Protocol (PPP) access is currently underway, which will allow direct access to university services without the need for terminal emulation.

OhioLINK is a cooperative effort among the 15 state-supported universities in Ohio and two private libraries—the State Library of Ohio and Case Western Reserve University in Cleveland. The project, along with three remote storage centers constructed in various parts of the state, was initiated to encourage the sharing of resources among universities and help alleviate the need for additional library space on every campus. For OhioLINK to be successful several prerequisites had to be established: 1) each participating library had to adopt the same library system, Innovative Interfaces, Inc. (III), headquartered in Emeryville, California, 2) a cite had to be chosen to house the Central Catalog and other databases that were to be made available to users, and 3) each campus had to be fully networked and have access to the Internet. The Central Catalog is located at Wright State University in Dayton, Ohio. Each member library has its own local catalog and contributes up to 95% of its online bibliographic, serial, and order information to the Central Catalog for sharing purposes.

The University's first online catalog ran from a computer housed in the library and was maintained almost completely by library staff. With the introduction of III and OhioLINK, library and Computer Center directors and staff agreed that it would be best to house the mainframe for the system (ZipLINK) at the Computer Center. Computer Center staff were familiar with DEC equipment, Ultrix mainframes, and, with the heavy reliance on networked services, would be able to better service the libraries and the system if the computer were located in the Computer Center.

Because OARnet was already in existence and much networking had been done on campus, the library's task of preparing for OhioLINK was much simplified. The biggest job was wiring the libraries internally; the main library and science library were both built in the late 1960s/early 1970s. Neither facility was constructed with networking in mind. Computer Center staff dedicated countless hours to the libraries—installing terminal servers, changing connectors on lines that had been used for hard-wired connections to the old system computer, installing new network lines, upgrading PCs to accommodate network demands, and learning about the special needs of libraries in the networked world.

As a result of all this work and effort, the University of Akron's library system is now a full and active member of OhioLINK. We were the sixth library in the state to be loaded to the Central Catalog. When the intercampus borrowing module of OhioLINK (P-Circ) went live in February 1994, the library was on the leading edge of campuses to begin to utilize the program. Each month the number of books shipped to and sent from the University of Akron's libraries—with most books reaching their destination within three days—grows. Well over 1000 books are received for Akron patrons each month and the same number are shipped from our libraries to other campuses in Ohio.

Patron access to the OhioLINK Central Catalog is provided in several ways. From within the libraries, users may automatically transfer searches from the local catalog to the Central Catalog or they may connect directly to OhioLINK Central from a menu option without logging into the local catalog. To simplify the process of connecting to OhioLINK Central for university patrons who are not in the library, access is provided through the University's campus information service—Campuserve (the local campus gopher). Students, staff, and faculty are able to select OhioLINK from a menu and be automatically connected to the service, thus eliminating the need to provide special access instructions to campus users. Also, to complement access to OhioLINK from Campuserve, all terminals located in the university libraries provide access to Campuserve. The menu structure of Campuserve was designed with much input from library personnel.

The Computing and Communications Technology Committee, a subcommittee of the University Faculty Senate, recently recommended that the university libraries be designated the "owner" of general information on campus, including Campuserve and Usenet News, and any future general information services (such as WWW) that may be developed. The belief is that Computer Center personnel are not trained for and do not have expertise in the legalities and politics of general information management; university libraries personnel are trained for and have experience in the collection and dissemination of information. While final approval of this proposal still must be made by the Faculty Senate, the Dean of Libraries and the Vice President for Information Services have agreed that the proposal is an excellent one. Technical support for all networked information services will continue to be the responsibility of the Computer Center.

Now that the base layer of the OhioLINK project is complete (there are many more services in development) and additional network information services have been established, it is gratifying and yet sometimes difficult to sit back and see the library users take OhioLINK so much for granted. The years of planning and months working to install all of the components were all for this one end: to better serve the user. What we librarians and computer specialists have learned is that the days of segregation are over. We can no longer afford to have one or two staff people in the library responsible for the "library's computer," and we can no longer have one or two Computer Center staff familiar with the library installation. Every library enhancement and every Computer Center advancement are irrevocably linked; we are definitely a team.

Areas of Cooperation Between the Library and Computing

Terri Fishel
Head of Reference, DeWitt Wallace Library
fishel@macalstr.edu

Peg Shultz
Assistant Director, Academic Computing & Information Technology
schultz@macalstr.edu

Macalester College

Faculty Workshops – May 1994

Computing and Information Technology (CIT) planned a series of workshops for faculty the week after graduation, when faculty are still on campus. The workshops included a component for the library, which focused on searching electronic information sources such as FirstSearch and UnCover, and also some basic information about locating discipline-specific electronic journals on Gopher and Mosaic. CIT covered basics such as email, gophers, and Mosaic. We also arranged to do follow-ups to the workshops by having teams (one person from the library and one from computing) visit participants' offices and discuss any problems or training issues. We had a very favorable response.

New Student Orientation – Fall 1994

The library has offered a hands-on session for new students for the past few years to introduce them to the online library catalog and other electronic library services during orientation week. This program has become increasingly successful and last year (fall 1993) more than half of the new students participated in the activities. The library and CIT have spent the last year meeting to develop a more in-depth program that will include both units in the orientation program.

This fall the library staff combined with CIT staff to expand the annual library orientation session for new students to include an introduction to the campus network. With the cooperation of computing, we were able to develop a series of exercises that introduced students not only to the electronic library resources but also provided hands-on opportunities in the computer lab, which allowed students to activate their VAX accounts and set their passwords and locate the short course registration list that allows users to register for workshops offered in the fall by CIT and the library. Four hundred of the five hundred incoming students attended one of the two sessions offered and the cooperation of computing made this the most successful orientation event we've ever had.

We continued to cooperate with computing in developing short courses throughout the fall semester and have combined to team-teach a session on Mosaic. We are currently developing another staff workshop and preparing short courses for the spring semester.

BUILDING A TEAM-BASED, INTEGRATED INFORMATION SERVICES ORGANIZATION

Joy Hughes
Associate Provost for Information Services
hughesj@ccmail.orst.edu

Charlene Grass
Associate University Librarian for Technology and Automation
grassc@ccmail.orst.edu

Oregon State University

In January 1994, Oregon State University created a new organizational unit, Information Services (IS), comprised of the libraries, computer services, media services, and telecommunications. The new unit is under the leadership of the associate provost for Information Services.

In March, eight interdepartmental teams were formed to investigate "hot issues." These issues represented areas that appeared likely candidates for reorganization because of apparent duplication or gaps in service. The issues were training and instruction, multimedia, Novell LAN support, front-line user services, instructional labs, large-scale systems, equipment repair and maintenance, and administrative functions. While these teams were meeting, a ninth team traveled the state of Oregon, meeting with OSU extension faculty who are based in county offices to explore how IS could assist these faculty in providing better services to their customers.

The nine teams met at an all-day, off-campus retreat to present their findings to one other. The teams made some modifications and then presented their findings to all of IS. Two strategic reorganization teams were then formed to synthesize the reports and make recommendations about how IS should reorganize to improve efficiency and service.

The associate provost analyzed the reports and designed an organizational structure to support the common themes and to address problems identified by the teams. She chose among alternative recommendations on the basis of how well the recommendation would facilitate the goals expressed by the teams and/or would address the problems identified by the teams.

The Plan

The plan is to create a team-based organization with fluid boundaries so that IS staff are not locked into ways of behaving, into a narrowly defined set of services, or into technologies, and thus are more able to approach the ideal of the "learning organization." This is an ambitious undertaking and will likely take three or four years to accomplish.

Once the plan is fully implemented, there will be no more departments in IS, and all IS front-line staff will be located in the new Library and Information Center.

The reorganization plan has been presented to OSU's President, the President's Cabinet, the University Quality Council, and the Deans' Group. The support of these influential groups is a tribute to the quality of the work of the many IS people who invested so much time and intelligence in the process.

The Transition

During the 1994-95 academic year, IS will be making the transition to "stage 1" of the reorganization. Stage 1 features a mix of teams and traditional departments. Library technical services, for example, will function about the same as it does now, whereas much of library public services will be reorganized into teams, with team members drawn from the library, computer services, telecommunications, and media services.

While the effort to move to stage 1 in just one year is considerable and challenging, it is also do-able. An interdepartmental transition team is guiding the process.

A few examples of the many stage 1 changes are as follows:

1. Administration: Currently each IS department has its own administrative service unit, providing accounting, purchasing, billing, and personnel services. The library has a

fundraising office. Media services does some grant development. Telecommunications offers some business services, such as telephone resale. These services will be centralized, thus making all of the services available to all departments. Fundraising, for example, will be able to discuss comprehensive technology needs with donors, not just library needs. We also expect to realize efficiencies that will enable us to dedicate more of our resources to supporting the University's strategic goals.

2. Consulting Services: This department will be team based and include staff drawn from the library, media services, computing services, and telecommunications. It will enable the integration of IS's help desk and front-line support activities. When the new Library and Information Center opens in a few years, these folks and most of the media development staff will be located in the new building.

Ongoing Cooperative Projects

Cooperative efforts among the departments are not waiting for the formal reorganization. For example, all four departments cooperated in the writing of a grant to network the extension offices. Library and computer services staff are working with extension services to explore cataloging extension documents and publishing these electronically. The library and computer services people involved in Internet training are co-designing an instructional video.

The telecommunications department has asked media services to manage its new interactive video services. All four departments are cooperating in putting forth a proposal to a vendor to field-test wireless technologies. An interdepartmental multimedia development team has been formed and is assisting faculty with the identification and evaluation of commercially published multimedia software and with the integration of the software into the curriculum.

Most important, the university librarian worked with computer services, media services, and telecommunications to redo the design for the new Library and Information Center so that the building can better support the plan for a team-based, integrated information services organization.

Consolidation, Centralization, Connections, and Cooperation at Indiana State University

Ron G. Martin
Associate for Library Services
libmart@cml.indstate.edu

H. Scott Davis
Head, Library Information Services Department
libdavi@cml.indstate.edu

M.K. "Chat" Chatterji
Interim Associate Director, User Services, Academic Computing and Networking Services
chat@pennylane.indstate.edu

Roseann Toulson
Associate Director, Technical Support, Academic Computing and Network Services
cccrat@amber.indstate.edu

Indiana State University

In November 1993, Indiana State University created the position of Associate Vice President for Information Services. The current Dean of Library Services was appointed to this position, to which the Library, Computing Services and Facilities (CSF), and Telecommunications subsequently reported. Before this time, these services did not serve under a common administrator. The goal of creating this "umbrella" position was to improve the delivery of information services to students, faculty, administrators, and staff in the support of learning, instruction, research, public service, and the day-to-day work of all Indiana State University personnel. More specific objectives were to accomplish the following:

1. better coordinate and integrate units providing information services and supporting information technologies that make up the campus information infrastructure,

2. improve services through collaborative efforts of personnel in the information services units , and

3. implement a long-range planning process for information technology needs for the campus.

While there had been occasional collaborative efforts among the three units, the intent of bringing the units under one administrator was to encourage, indeed mandate, stronger cooperative working relationships and recognize that all three units were integrally connected in the area of Information Services. The new administrative structure was achieved without adding more staff.

Though this new structure has been in place less than one year, several initiatives already have been undertaken to fulfill the goals and objectives of Information Services:

1. Immediately, the new Associate Vice President for Information Services formed several advisory committees, with wide representation from various constituencies on campus.

2. All academic units and areas on campus for which vice presidents are responsible (e.g., Academic Affairs, Business Affairs, Student Affairs, University Advancement, etc.) developed multiyear plans that identified the future needs for information services. These plans are critical to the development of strategic plans for the three units (Library, CSF, and Telecommunications), not to mention the overall strategic plan for Information Services.

3. Staff from the three units have worked together closely to coordinate and clarify a campus-wide information services training program, taking advantage of the expertise within the various units.

4. The various staffs have worked together to identify technical strengths and weaknesses of computer hardware and software and have defined clearer and more efficient responsibilities in this area.

5. The three units have had joint meetings in which staff were able to get acquainted with their colleagues and learn more about the services offered in each area.

6. Specialized teams have also been formed, with more to be appointed later, in the areas of communications and publications. An Information Services communications team has been formed, comprising members from each of the units in Information Services. The team's charge is to draft an ongoing communications program, with both short-term activities and long-term initiatives. And a publications team has been formed to produce a joint newsletter, again made up of members from the various units.

So far, a number of administrative changes have occurred, some as a direct result of the new reporting relationship, and some not. Following is an organization chart for FY 1994/95 showing what the organization looks like now. More changes will likely occur, as the new arrangement is operational and periodically submitted to assessment and evaluation. However, informal reports to date are positive as Indiana State University positions itself for its information needs, for both now and the future.

Indiana State University
Current Combined Organization Chart, FY 1994–95

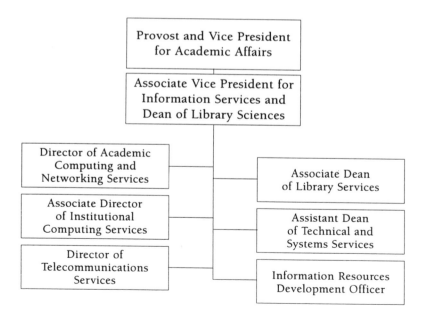

AN OPPORTUNITY: COOPERATION
BETWEEN THE LIBRARY AND COMPUTER SERVICES

James L. Mullins
Director of Library Services, Franklin D. Schurz Library,
Indiana University South Bend
jmullins%library%iusb@vines.iusb.indiana.edu

About 12 years ago, on the campus of Indiana University South Bend, the library was the only "game in town." It had little competition for nonpersonnel funds, making it possible for the library to gain support from the faculty and administration for increases to the materials and equipment budgets. Then the impact of computerization/technology made itself felt. Along with other units on campus, the library became an avid user of computers and the new technology. This use of technology eventually developed into a dependency that could not be denied by either Computer Services or the library. At the beginning of the 1990s, the library and Computer Services were poised for a struggle to maintain the funding necessary to meet present and future service demands.

Several years ago, it became apparent to the administrators of Computer Services and the library that they would both benefit by working together to help meet each other's needs, rather than compete for a limited "pot of gold."

The first instance of cooperation came when the need for additional student computer labs arose on campus. The Schurz Library opened in 1989 with a well-equipped media facility. After two years, it was becoming apparent that the media center was not being used to its potential and that the space was being underutilized.

The directors of the library and the Computer Center met and reviewed the space. They determined that an 18-station computer lab could be located in the media center. (The media equipment was subsequently integrated into the visual aid resource room.) A small office was given to the lab supervisor and the computer lab opened.

In short order, it was the most popular computer lab on campus due to its beautiful surroundings and long hours.

After two years, few problems have developed concerning the lab. The library faculty and staff are happy to have it housed within the library, and the Computer Services staff is pleased to have been able to find an already furnished central location.

Another point of cooperation between Computer Services and the library staffs has been instructing students, faculty, and staff on the use of the Internet. A year ago, the Computer Services staff saw the primary responsibility for providing access to the Internet as their own. When it appeared to the librarians that nothing was happening to educate the faculty about the available Internet resources, the librarians decided it was time to take action. Several librarians devised an instructional method for teaching faculty about Internet resources and ways to access them.

Some problems soon developed. Computer services staff felt the library staff were infringing on their responsibilities. The librarians countered that information was their responsibility to access whether it was in a book, periodical, microform, CD-ROM, or a remote database. After a while, this argument seemed logical to the campus administration and Computer Services staff.

After further discussion, it was decided that Internet training could easily be divided between the two staffs. The library would take the responsibility for teaching about the types of databases available and how to reach them. The Computer Services staff would assist in making the technical connections necessary as well as instructing in such areas as File Transfer Protocol (FTP). The librarians and Computer Services staff developed a workshop for the faculty and, within one day of its announcement, it was filled. This scheme worked well throughout the spring of 1994. It is also the way in which Internet training is being conducted during the 1994/95 academic year.

The working relationship between Computer Services and Schurz Library has grown stronger during the past several years. Much of the success is due to the clarification of which responsibilities are whose. Less time is spent on turf battles and more time is spent providing a coherent approach to information resources—whether in-house or located a thousand miles away.

Documents to the People: A Collaborative Approach

James Ostlund
Director, User Services, Office of University Computing
james.j.ostlund.1@nd.edu

Maureen Gleason
Deputy Director, Hesburgh Library
mgleason@vma.cc.nd.edu

University of Notre Dame

Three years ago the University Libraries of Notre Dame identified a problem that was interfering with user access to an important part of the collections. It was, however, a problem that the libraries could not solve alone. At the same time, the Office of University Computing was seeking ways to employ technology creatively in support of education and research at Notre Dame. The two objectives converged and a potential solution was jointly proposed.

In 1886, the federal government established the Federal Depository System to provide government publications to its citizens. Since that time, depository libraries like the University of Notre Dame have been assisting the general public in selecting and using government information in paper and microfiche formats. In 1990, the Government Printing Office (GPO) began distributing government information in Compact Disc-Read Only Memory (CD-ROM) format to the depository libraries. Although well received, CD-ROMs have presented the many depository libraries with a new and difficult challenge: how to provide to the general public quality access to government information comparable to that which has been their tradition for many years.

Libraries, while expert and conversant with CD technology in the form of bibliographic files, for example, indexes and abstracts from the private sector, are inexperienced in providing traditional services to the newer electronic products such as numeric datafiles, full-text files, and graphics using distributed connectivity technology. In the case of depository CDs, this is further complicated by the uncoordinated nature of the distribution process. The GPO distributes what the federal agencies provide. Hence, each CD product may have different software, operating systems, and structure. Additionally, CD services within a library traditionally have been in a small stand-alone workstation or a Local Area Network (LAN), which serves only that one library or building and requires frequent changing of the CDs themselves. Access to remote users via dial- up access of other forms of connectivity are not the traditional form of service.

A collaborative effort between the Hesburgh Library and the Office of University Computing was established and completed on the University of Notre Dame campus. This effort resulted in a grant request to the U.S. government in the form of a Research and Demonstration Project. The following abstract is reproduced from that grant proposal:

> CD-ROM is now the preferred format for the publication of government data, but it is inaccessible to the average citizen for a number of reasons. Sophisticated hardware and software are required; application programs are difficult to use and limited in scope; and the sheer number of discs involved makes for significant problems in handling. The CD-ROM Research & Demonstration Project for U. S. Government Data intends to develop new tools to facilitate end-users' access to CD data files; expand the interface beyond the DOS environment to other platforms; eliminate the problems of handling hundreds of discs by using storage devices designed for that purpose; facilitate movement of data to other platforms for specialized analysis; and provide state, regional and national access via networks. The goals of the project are to decrease the time end-users must spend to access these CD-ROMs, significantly increase the general accessibility of these data, develop recommended system guidelines and formats and identify areas for future research.

Unfortunately, the proposal, although favorably reviewed and ranking high among the submissions, was not funded. The experience of developing it, however, educated both library and computer staff and provided the groundwork for future collaboration.

Library Explorer: Information Skills, Strategies, and Sources

Janice Simmons-Welburn
Head, Main Library, Information & Instructional Department,
and Coordinator, Systemwide Reference Services
j-simmons-welburn@uiowa.edu

Marsha Forys
Reference Librarian, Coordinator for Instructional Services
marsha-forys@uiowa.edu

The University of Iowa

Library Explorer is a computer-assisted instruction (CAI) program designed to engage students in independent, self-directed learning. Library Explorer uses a book metaphor. A button located beside the book onscreen directs the user to the table of contents, glossary, and index, and enables the user to turn pages, go to a specific page, and mark pages of interest. There is also a "help" button. Throughout the text, students are able to click on "hot" words to get definitions.

The University of Iowa Libraries staff obtained support for Library Explorer's development through the Instructional Computing Award Program, a yearly grant competition conducted by Weeg Computing Center with the assistance of the University of Iowa Computer-Based Education Committee. The award granted to the Libraries gave them full software development assistance through all phases of development from staff in Weeg's Instructional Software Development Group (ISDG).

From the beginning, the planning for and the development of computer-assisted instruction at the Libraries has had an element of groups and partnerships.

The Computer-Assisted Instruction Task Force, which studied the feasibility of CAI and made various recommendations, was made up of several librarians from throughout the system and one person from Weeg.

Library Explorer was the result of partnerships between the Libraries, Weeg Computing Center, and the Rhetoric Department. (Rhetoric courses, an integration of speaking, reading, and writing, are part of the General Education Requirement at the University of Iowa and are taken by most freshmen and some transfer students.) In the initial stages, the group working on Library Explorer comprised three librarians from various departments who served as content experts, one Libraries staff member with expertise in instructional design and software development, one faculty member from the Rhetoric Department, and two software developers from the Instructional Software Development Group in Weeg who have instructional design and software development expertise. At the script writing stage, two more librarians were brought in so that the three chapters of the program would be worked on by teams of two. Chapter one's team consisted of a librarian and a Rhetoric Department faculty member, and chapters two and three were worked on by teams of librarians. During the implementation stage, the two original software developers were helped by others in their department, and they drew on other University staff as well when they needed a photographer and a graphic artist. The maintenance phase will involve librarians, who will monitor the accuracy of the content, and a member of the Information Arcade staff, who will update the program as needed.

A university library can be a complex, overwhelming place, and Library Explorer was created to make it all seem less complicated, in an interactive, visually appealing way. Library Explorer enables us to reach a larger percentage of students we were not able to reach previously. Library Explorer provides users with accurate information at a point of need and allows independent, self-paced learning.

Library Explorer aids users in

1. identifying appropriate types of information sources for their research topics;

2. finding pertinent books using OASIS' LCAT, the University of Iowa Libraries' online catalog, and the card catalog;

3. finding periodical and newspaper articles with electronic indexes such as OASIS' WILS, *The MLA Bibliography* on CD-ROM, the *Des Moines Register Index* on CD-ROM, and print

indexes and abstracts such as *The Readers' Guide to Periodical Literature, Sage Family Studies Abstracts,* and *The New York Times Index;*

4. determining whether the University of Iowa Libraries owns a copy of a particular book or periodical; and

5. locating a book or periodical on library shelves.

The partnership between the Libraries, the Instructional Software Development Group from the Weeg Computing Center, and the Rhetoric Department has resulted in a highly effective, visually appealing product that helps students learn various information gathering skills. All of the parties involved developed a better understanding and appreciation of our respective roles in supporting undergraduate education at the University. The members of the Computing Center staff frequently comment on how their knowledge of the library has increased and look forward to working with us on future projects. The Libraries staff also found this partnership to be a rewarding experience and value the Computing Center staff as colleagues.

UCI Libraries Internet Information Access via World-Wide Web

Lorelei Tanji
Fine Arts Librarian, University of California, Irvine
ltanji@uci.edu

The UCI Libraries and the Office of Academic Computing (OAC), in recognition of their joint roles as information providers, collaborated on an Internet/X Terminal project to expand and optimize use of Internet resources in order to enhance support of research and instruction for faculty, staff, and students at the University of California, Irvine.

Shirley Leung, Assistant University Librarian for Research and Instructional Services, formed a committee of seven library staff, with experience in reference, systems, and discipline-related subject areas (fine arts, humanities, social sciences, government/law, and sciences) to work on this project. The Office of Academic Computing's participation was coordinated by Stephen Franklin, Director of Advanced Scientific Computing. This participation included the loan of eight X terminals, and more important, substantial technical support from various OAC staff.

The committee met for the first time on December 10, 1993. They were given the charge to explore the capabilities of X terminals and the power of X-Mosaic software to facilitate the multimedia retrieval and presentation of Internet sources. OAC staff acted as consultants and partners in this project.

By the beginning of January 1994, each committee member had an X terminal to practice on. After familiarizing themselves with X terminals, Motif Window manager software, and Mosaic software, the committee members began to compile lists of significant Internet resources to highlight on a UCI Libraries Home Page. By March, the committee had developed a training program and provided hands-on workshops to all interested library staff (50 people) from both public services and technical services on the use of X terminals and Mosaic searching. (Each workshop was 2 hours long, limited to 3 people.)

Jonathan Cohen, a graduate student who had created a Web site for the UCI Campus Bookstore, was hired part time to assist in the creation of the UCI Libraries Web site. The committee decided to create a subject-specific Home Page that could be utilized in Internet workshops for faculty, students, and staff. Working with the Library Information Systems Department, OAC staff, and Jonathan Cohen, the committee dealt with various technical issues for public access such as security to the server, telnet access and use implications, restriction of hosts, the suppression of certain functions (i.e., printing), automatic login with the Home Page, time-out functions, and the future possibility of a form for submitting online user surveys.

By April, some of the X terminals were moved to public service desks (Information, Reference, and Government Publications Reference). Staff at these desks began to take advantage of the multitasking ability to access multiple sessions of OPACs and to incorporate the use of Mosaic in their service. By May, and with appropriate campus publicity, the rest of the X terminals were moved to the lobby of the Main Library and were available for use by the UCI community.

The completed Home Page provided easy access to interesting Internet sources arranged by broad disciplines. User surveys, comment books, and binders containing instructions, FAQs (frequently asked questions), and Internet guides were placed next to each workstation. The committee had also developed a script for teaching Internet workshops to the UCI community. In conjunction with OAC trainers and other bibliographers who had received Mosaic training, the committee members gave these workshops in an OAC computer lab that allowed for hands-on training. Initially, two workshops were offered for each of the following areas: fine arts, humanities, social sciences, science/technology/medicine, and law/government/business. By popular demand, an additional six workshops were opened with a total of approximately 105 participants. Attendees represented a wide range of faculty, students, and staff—some with no computer experience and others with Gopher Internet experience. It is hoped that UCI community members will begin to incorporate these resources in their teaching and research and that exposure to the World-Wide Web will inspire them to create future Internet resources.

Some of the positive outcomes of this project are 1) a closer tie between the UCI Libraries and the Office of Academic Computing; 2) the creation of a UCI Libraries Home Page that highlights Internet resources of interest to the UCI community; 3) public access to the Home Page on X terminals in the Main Library lobby; 4) the development of workshops on Mosaic and the World-Wide Web to teach Internet navigation skills to the public and staff; 5) increased proficiency in the library staff about networked information environments and Internet searching; and 6) the use of X terminals at some public service desks.

The collaboration enabled the UCI Libraries to move into the forefront of networked information technology in a relatively short time. With the success of this collaboration, both the UCI Libraries and OAC are poised to implement enhanced or new service programs to the UCI community and anticipate future training in the many departmental computer labs on campus and an increase in the provision of outreach consultation and research services.

Appendix 3

CREATING A VIRTUAL INFORMATION ORGANIZATION: COLLABORATIVE
RELATIONSHIPS BETWEEN LIBRARIES AND COMPUTING CENTERS
Sheila D. Creth, University of Iowa

The article on the following pages was originally published in
Journal of Library Administration, Vol. 19, No. 3/4, 1993, 111–132.
It is reprinted here with permission of Haworth Press.

Enrollees were asked to read this paper before coming to the Institute.

CREATING A VIRTUAL INFORMATION ORGANIZATION: COLLABORATIVE RELATIONSHIPS BETWEEN LIBRARIES AND COMPUTING CENTERS

Sheila D. Creth

University Librarian, University of Iowa

Phrases such as "information age," "global information economy," are ones that appear with considerable frequency in a variety of contexts including in library professional literature and the popular media. The very frequency of such terms, as applied to computer-based technology and communication systems, and to organizational strategies and structure, may have dulled our alertness to the magnitude of the fundamental changes that are emerging while also clouding our ability to see clearly what is indeed changing and what remains essentially the same.

There is, of course, no "age" that has not depended on information as a basic element in all aspects of society, including as the underpinning of the economy. What is the difference, then, in today's world that such hyperbole is applied to information and, more specifically, information technology? Since the mid 1980s a transformation has occurred in which information itself has become a primary economic commodity rather than a means by which products and services are exchanged, bartered or sold. Drucker, using information and knowledge interchangeably, described the current and future society as one in which "knowledge is the primary resource for individuals and for the economy overall. . . . the purpose and function of every organization, business and non-business alike, is the integration of specialized knowledge into a common task." [1]

Information technology has created an interactive and expansive quality to information not experienced previously thus contributing to information becoming a primary commodity. Information is no longer static. Instead it can be continually added to, growing in value as the original data, message or idea is augmented. In addition, the speed and connections of networks have opened channels of communication within organizations and across organizational boundaries and provided a "real time" sense of communication among people distributed around the world. Information technology has created a sense of urgency and created new possibilities for product development and delivery of services. At the same time, the impact of information technology in communication processes and connections challenges basic assumptions about organization structure, working relationships and the nature and quality of services.

The reality, then, is that whatever labels — information age, global information village — are used to describe the current environment, all organizations are faced with finding ways to respond effectively and innovatively to a very different landscape in meeting user/customer expectations and competition from whatever source, in order to survive and even flourish.

The economic pressures and competitive realities are no less real for universities, and maybe more so, as these historically conservative institutions seek ways to respond to a rapidly changing environment. Among the many tensions that permeate higher education are a decline in student enrollments, diminished funding support from the federal government both in grants and indirect cost payments, and increased demands for accountability by the public regarding fees, costs and the quality of education. Universities have a major opportunity to respond rapidly and innovatively to exploit the full power of information technology for scholarly research, teaching and independent learning.

A recent paper on information technology, developed for university presidents by the Higher Education Information Resources Alliance, stated that "like it or not, prepared or not, our institutions of higher education are entering the information age. We have experienced more than a decade of proliferation of personal computers on the desks of executives, administrators, faculty, and students; of widely extended access to research resources, teaching techniques, administrative databases, and colleagues across campus and the world. Most institutions report increasing pressure from various constituencies for access to the power they believe to be available through the information technologies; instant answers, process shortcuts, responsiveness to individual needs, cost savings. . . . This is the time . . . to effect the real information technology revolution; adjusting our organizational structures to accommodate and exploit what is valuable in these technological developments." [2]

Libraries and computer centers are the two organizations within higher education that can provide leadership and create new directions for the campus through the application of information technology. They also have the most to lose. In order to be leaders — and not losers — librarians and computer professionals will have to be willing to make fundamental changes in all aspects of their roles and responsibilities, skills and knowledge, working relationships and organization cultures. By aggressively exploring opportunities to work collaboratively to deliver services including wholly new services, librarians and computer professionals can exploit the full potential of information technology in innovative and timely ways.

Traditional Relationship between Libraries and Computer Centers

Most typically, the relationship between academic librarians and computer professionals has been one characterized by unease, caution, lack of knowledge and understanding, and occasionally outright mistrust. Over the past two decades, a small number of professionals from both organizations have worked together successfully, but it has been a relationship based on the library "purchasing" services from the computing center — programming, computer time on the mainframe, technical advice and support. During the late 1970s and throughout the 1980s, the services purchased focused on the development or installation of an online library system (i.e., automated public catalog, circulation and acquisition systems). More recently, commercially produced databases have been mounted on the mainframe as part of the online library system, along with locally developed information databases such as "news" services. The library's relationship with the computing center has been basically no different than the relationship between the computing center and the admissions office, the registrar's office or other campus academic or administrative units that depend on the technical services of the computing center. The library administration contracted with the computing administration for services, and then the staff of the two organizations worked together to carry out the project to be accomplished.

The power, proliferation and complexity of today's information technology suggests that more than this traditional working relationship is not only possible, but essential. During the mid-1980s, a number of articles which focused on the administrative merger of academic libraries and computing centers began to appear.[3] These articles presented opinions and views about how the increasingly re-

lated and/or overlapping responsibilities of librarians and computing professionals would be handled in the future through administrative mergers. Some articles contained prophetic statements and
even an occasional misleading statement about "trends" regarding
such mergers. Primarily, however, these articles missed the point
because they focused on administrative structure and control (who
would win the struggle for perceived dominance and power on campus), rather than on a process for capitalizing on the combined
knowledge of both professional groups. The issue of administrative
control pales in comparison to the more fundamental issue of what
might be, and should be, accomplished with information technology if library and computing professionals were to combine their
expertise in activities such as strategic planning, developing campus information policy, offering educational programs, designing
knowledge management systems, and providing greater support to
faculty for curriculum development. Now that concern with administrative mergers seems to no longer be of primary concern, the field
is clear for professionals to give attention to what is really needed:
developing a commitment to creating a truly collaborative culture
in which librarians and computer professionals work together to
develop mutual projects and a support structure to achieve a flexible and innovative response to the integration of information technology into all aspects of university life.

Collaborative Relationships; Virtual Organizations

In his book, *Shared Minds: The New Technologies of Collaboration*,
Schrage explored the similarities and difference among communication, cooperation and collaboration, and how the expansion of
information technology offers a unique opportunity for individuals
and organizations to focus on collaboration. Schrage defined collaboration as an "act of shared creation and/or shared discovery".[4]
He drew a sharp distinction between collaboration and communication — the exchange of information, and cooperation — people
working together for a common purpose without necessarily having
defined the purpose.

The process of collaboration, according to Schrage, requires a different approach and set of expectations, and it is a process between
equals. Certainly not all situations require nor lend themselves to a
collaborative response. Schrage indicated that collaboration is distinguished by a "desire or need to solve a problem, create, or dis-
cover something within a set of constraints." He stated that collabo-

ration is not routine or predictable and is not an assembly-line process. Finally Schrage observed that the issue is not more communication or even teamwork, rather "it's the creation of value. Collaboration describes a process of value creation that our traditional structures of communication and teamwork can't achieve." [5]

This concept of collaboration and the key role it can play by building on opportunities available through communication technologies, supports the concept of the "virtual" organization. An extensive article in the February 1993 issue of *Business Week* could refer with a few word changes to university libraries and computing centers: "The virtual organization is a temporary network of independent companies — suppliers, customers, even erstwhile rivals — linked by information technology to share skills, costs, and access to one another's markets. It will have neither central office nor organization chart. It will have no hierarchy, no vertical integration. Instead . . . this new, evolving corporate model will be fluid and flexible — a group of collaborators that quickly unite to exploit a specific opportunity. Once the opportunity is met, the venture will, more often than not, disband." [6] The article went on to state that the virtual organization, with a foundation resting on the capacity of information technology and the communication superhighways, will have "partnering" as a key attribute.

The concept of a "virtual library" began to appear in the literature over the past several years with discussion focusing on creating shared collections and services among libraries in a consortium. Most recently the Association of Research Libraries issued a SPEC kit on this topic demonstrating the currency this concept is enjoying even if actual application of the concept is not yet a reality. [7] Although it is encouraging to see this nascent discussion in the literature, it would be unfortunate if a singular focus on the virtual library diminished the opportunity for collaborative efforts of librarians and computer professionals. University libraries are likely to work more extensively with one another in a collaborative mode in the future. This interlibrary collaboration, however, should not replace the need to create the virtual information organization on individual campuses.

This model — a collaborative, virtual organization — not administrative merger, is more likely to generate a network of people who will be able to apply their expertise, knowledge and energy in directing the use of information technology to support the mission of the university.

Although most articles about the impact of information technology on organizational infrastructure have focused on the for-profit, corporate environment, there is every reason to apply the same concepts to campus library and computing center operations. Indeed, in the paper entitled "What Presidents Need to Know . . . about the Integration of Information Technologies on Campus," there is a clear call for what should be done to harness the power of current and emerging technologies. [8] The paper called for an examination of ways in which to add value to scholarship and teaching, and to develop "organizational, instruction, and informational infrastructures" by capitalizing on technologies.

Creating a collaborative environment, a virtual information organization, will be appealing to some. Many professionals, though, may resist making fundamental changes in all aspects of their work lives. Minimally, professionals will need to cultivate clear perceptions of their professional colleagues in the other organization, examine and revise as necessary their expectations regarding individual roles and responsibilities, and acquire a different set of knowledge and abilities in order to work effectively in an organization culture that is less structured, more ambiguous and in a constant state of change. Administrators will need to consider incentives to encourage such change.

Unless a highly fluid and flexible working environment is created, both libraries and computing centers risk a decline in their role in the university. Strangled by too few resources and unable to respond to the many and diverse expectations and demands for service and support, libraries and computing centers standing alone may indeed become the "white elephants" that some predict. Information technology promises to be one of the more powerful influences in the shape of higher education into the 21st century. Librarians and computer professionals working as partners can be major players in the innovative application of these technologies in support of the university's mission.

Realities for Computing Centers and Libraries

In the past several years, pressures on libraries and computing centers have mounted. Libraries have been struggling with runaway cost inflation for materials, the proliferation of new print publications, and a flood of materials now available in electronic formats. During this period, budgets for materials and staff as well as for computing hardware and software and other operational needs, have been squeezed and often reduced. These considerable budget pressures have occurred at a time when faculty and students are clamoring for more timely, easy, and convenient access to information resources (owned locally or obtained elsewhere), and for greater assistance in learning to understand and use the complexity of information resources.

Computing centers have been faced with their own set of difficulties including keeping up with the pace of change in technology, replacement of hardware and operating systems, creation of powerful networks on campus, distribution of personal computers in multiple locations across the campus, and the demand from users for support in learning how to effectively use the available technology. Although the costs of computing hardware and software continues to decline in price, these expenditures represent a major capital investment for universities and the funds have not been as readily available in the past few years as they were during the 1980s. In addition, the concept of campus computing being centrally administrated has evaporated with the proliferation of personal computers and local area networks throughout the university. Now the computing center staff must find ways to influence and direct campus computing developments even though they do not retain administrative control over the full range of computing systems and computing power in the university.

Both computing and library professionals have to work with limited, and often inadequate resources, in relation to the task before them. Rather than proceeding down similar and parallel paths, the staff of both units should join together as partners in order to meet the escalating demands of the campus community, and to provide local and national leadership in the design and shape of information technology and its application for learning and scholarship.

Characteristics of Libraries and Computing Centers

A first step in moving toward a collaborative environment is recognition of the current role, strengths and attributes of each organization and its professionals.

We would benefit from assessment that is based on comprehensive and current research. Such research is not available, though, the views of a number of authors are helpful in both highlighting the characteristics and acknowledging the misconceptions that undoubtedly still exist among librarians and computer professionals. Neff described the role of a library as primarily a repository with functions including acquiring, lending and borrowing of "organized packaged information". On the other hand, Neff saw the role of the computer center as suppling machines, procedures and people for activities that include inputting, manipulating, storing, retrieving and displaying information. He indicated that services in the computing center are not central to its role. [9] No doubt there are individuals who would take issue with Neff's limited understanding of the role of libraries and library professionals, not to mention his view that services are not central to a computing center.

Molholt, in her article entitled "Converging Paths: The Computing Center and the Library," described the characteristics of computing centers as providing twenty-four hour access, unlimited and cost effective storage, direct access to both local and remote data and easily manipulable files, and a high degree of technical expertise. She viewed library characteristics as complementary to those of the computer center by offering user friendly orientation, highly structured files and collections, a relative uniformity of access which obviates extensive user training, free access, and a high degree of subject expertise among staff. [10]

Battin offered a perspective that focused on goals to characterize the two organizations. She viewed librarians as being "at the center of the research process in our universities for the past century," while those in technology have "focused on highly specific disciplinary concerns, and tended to emphasize the capacities of the technology for a discrete avenue of research . . . rather than broader requirements of the scholarly community at large." [11]

Sack provided a more critical overview of the role of libraries and computer centers and saw similarities in the intrinsic characteristics of both organizations. He described both as hard to use, distant, rule-bound and inflexible. He suggested that both organizations are "devoted to a 'divide and complicate' philosophy when the best of scholarship tries to integrate and unify." [12]

Jones focused on the skills of the two professional groups. He described computer professionals as having skills in "system development and telecommunications; skills in product development . . . while librarians have good people interface skills, skills for organizing knowledge, and the skills for marketing, training and sales." Jones concluded by saying that computer professionals and librarians "could be a particularly productive team." [13]

If computer professionals and librarians are to be a productive team, they will need to develop a much clearer understanding of one another. This requires that they examine far more than activities and tasks, and categories of skills and knowledge. An understanding of the history, culture and values that exist within both organizations is essential if truly collaborative relationships are to emerge. A thorough assessment of the cultural aspects of each organization could lay the groundwork for respect and trust. It could also avoid what Dougherty has warned against when he states that "many important differences between libraries and computer centers do exist. To forget this is to invite the risk of oversimplifying the complexity of bringing about closer and better relations." [14]

Although this is not the place to explore the histories of the two professions, it is worthwhile to highlight aspects of the respective cultures and the values that shape the culture. In a program conducted by this author for a group of library and computing administrators and managers from the same university, participants addressed both culture and values within the two organizations. [15]

First, the participants indicated that computer professionals come from a variety of educational and experiential backgrounds. Since they do not share a common professional and academic preparation, there is no socialization process for a computer professional prior to accepting a position in a computer organization. They considered this lack of shared professional philosophy and values to be a major contributor to an ethos in which individual action and thought is more highly regarded than a focus on the views, standards or values of the collective group.

In contrast, this group of professionals considered that librarians with their similar educational backgrounds experience a process of acculturation in which they develop a shared philosophy and common values. Therefore, they are more likely to act within the boundaries of accepted professional beliefs and behavior, being less likely to act independently.

In a related exercise, the participants in this workshop identified some values that they believe to be associated more strongly with one or the other professional group and those that they considered were shared.

COMPUTING PROFESSIONALS	LIBRARIANS
technical orientation	service orientation
entrepreneurial behavior	consensus approach
creativity encouraged	fiscal responsibility

{ .... professional orientation .... }

{ .... focus on global information community .... }

{ .... concerned with well being of university .... }

This list, developed by one group of professionals and in a brief period of time, should be considered only as a place to begin to understand what values may be shared, what values might be in conflict, and what values might be complementary.

This process of examining culture and values would be a constructive exercise at every university with computing and library professionals discussing these issues together in order to achieve a better understanding and respect for one another. It is time to remove the barriers that limit the ability of professionals to work effectively together, to overcome what Battin has stated as the "respective images of each other that continue to keep us apart." [16]

Shaping the Virtual Information Organization Through Information Technology

The very technology that is the "stuff" of computing center and library professional life provides the tools and process for redesigning the organization to create the collaborative, virtual organization. Redesigning the organization to introduce greater simplicity and flexibility is a significant challenge, and no less so in a university environment in which administrators tend to protect their turf and the status quo, rather than explore new designs that might alter their administrative control. But the pressure on the individuals who are struggling to keep up with the demands of today's environment requires new ways of accomplishing work. The redesign of the organization is imperative.

Keen stated that "globalization has extended lines of communication and coordination across time zones and locations, affecting breadth of markets, services, customer demands . . . This hyper-extension of activities is greatly straining the ability of traditional organizations to respond." [17] He went on to indicate that pressures are increasing due to the stress of "shortened planning, development and delivery cycles, and increased environmental volatility have drastically reduced acceptable reaction time." [18]

Organizational complexity is reflected, according to Keen, in more managerial layers, elaboration of procedures and controls, administrative overhead, reliance on communication by paper and reporting systems. This complexity finally contributes to a sluggish organization in both quality and timeliness of response in a constantly changing environment. Universities are large complex organizations, as are libraries and computing centers.

Drucker stated that the management of the "new organization" has to draw on three systematic practices. First, pursue a continuing improvement of every thing the organization does; second, learn to exploit organization knowledge and development of the next generation of applications from its successes; and, finally, learn to plan innovation and change in a systematic way. Drucker believed that a high degree of decentralization was necessary to achieve this organizational change. [19]

Keen also considered change as a norm for the collaborative organization but indicated that what is required to respond to this new norm is "a shift in emphasis from organizing by division of labor to organizing by division of knowledge." He considered that the division of knowledge "captures an obvious reality of work in an era of rapid change and uncertainty. Tasks are no longer predictable and experience may no longer be valuable. New inputs of knowledge are needed to define tasks, and multiple skills and experience are needed to complete them." [20]

By exploiting the range of information technology to create "rich and dense connections," it is possible to reconceptualize the relationships within and between computing center and library professionals. If the construct of a virtual information organization is the template that guides thinking and action, it will be possible to establish new, exciting and challenging opportunities for truly collaborative and innovative actions. Actions that focus on the users of information resources and technology, and the use of "computing to enhance good education." [21]

Opportunities in the Virtual Information Organization

There are a number of issues and activities that require immediate attention in universities that would be most effectively addressed through a partnership between computer and library professionals and the involvement of other parties such as faculty. The following six project categories are certainly not exhaustive of the possibilities that exist on individual campuses and nationally, but any one of the following would represent a significant beginning.

Strategic Planning

Librarians and computer professionals simply must begin to map out their future directions and priorities together. The library is no longer a user or consumer of computing resources similar to other administrative or academic units on campus. The library as a provider of access to information resources is at the very core of the university's mission, and, with the expansion into electronic resources and heavy reliance on information technology, the library is at the core of the computer center's future as well. With increased integration and dependance on information technology, library managers cannot afford to be surprised by decisions about computing support on campus and, in fact, they should be intimately involved in planning for long-term developments and resource allocation. Equally important, computing center managers should not be caught off guard by decisions that library managers make. The computing center managers should be involved in a collaborative manner in strategic decision-making about expanding information resources in electronic format, and major directions of information technology applications in the library. It is no longer adequate to "share information" with one another; we have to share, indeed develop, ideas and concepts together as part of a planning process.

Campus Information Policy

There is a range of information policy issues that require immediate and ongoing attention on campus and should be addressed in a number of forums in order to acquire sufficient views, opinions and, eventually, consensus. For example, every institution needs to have a well-defined policy regarding access to information for members of the university, with frank attention given to the liability of a "have" and "have not" information environment that could result from the costs and changes in funding mechanisms for electronic resources. [22]

Librarians and computer professionals should provide leadership to identify the issues and to facilitate focused discussions and tangible outcomes. By working collaboratively, the two professionals groups are likely to be more effective in recommending a course of action to central administration, as well as in suggesting a structure involving various constituencies to provide ongoing review of policy issues.

Knowledge Management Environment

The concept of libraries as knowledge management centers has been developed and implemented at the Johns Hopkins University Welch Medical Library and the University of California San Francisco Library. Lucier stated that a knowledge management environment "encompasses an integration of data and knowledge sources, access and delivery systems, education and training programs, and personalized services." [23]

The most unusual departure in this model is the primary emphasis on collaborative work with faculty that results in developing new information products and services in the form of knowledge databases. As Lucier pointed out, this model "insinuates the library at the beginning of the information transfer cycle rather than at the end and focuses on information capture rather than access and use." [24]

Librarians, with their knowledge of information organization, existing electronic resources and subject expertise, coupled with the range of technical skills represented by computer professionals, offer a rich resource that would be welcome by researchers to develop a knowledge management environment.

Support for Curriculum Development

The combined efforts of technologists and librarians could have a significant impact on the development of new approaches to instruction on university campuses. During the past five years, interest in using programs such as hypermedia to develop new approaches for teaching and learning have spread rapidly in colleges and universities. To date, though, developments have been achieved primarily through the efforts and enthusiasm of individual faculty, rather than through established university programs that promote and support such developments. If there is to be substantial integration of information technology into teaching, significant resources need to be made available to support faculty in this effort.

The University of Iowa has demonstrated the capacity to create significant change in curriculum through the collaborative efforts of faculty, librarians and computer professionals. The Information Arcade, located in the Main Library, is a facility that supports teaching, research and independent learning through technology and electronic information resources. The facility consists of an electronic classroom with twenty-six workstations that are fully networked and an additional fifty-six workstations including multi-media equipment.

What makes this facility so unusual is the manner in which it was conceived and developed. Over a period of two years, a small group of librarians, faculty and computer professionals discussed ways in which the use of information technology in teaching and research could be more aggressively encouraged and supported. From these many discussions arose the concept of an electronic information facility that would include a classroom for teaching, workstations for learning and exploring electronic resources, and a cadre of people with technological and information expertise to provide assistance and support to faculty and students.

Together, this group developed a proposal that resulted in a three-year grant of $752,000 from an Iowa foundation combined with significant support from the University administration. In order to maintain the collaborative foundation of this project beyond the initial concept, a structure was put in place to promote continued active collaboration into the design and operation of the Arcade during its initial years. A Steering Committee, consisting of the University Librarian, the Director of the Office of Information Technology, and a senior faculty member who was involved in the original conceptualizing and planning, provides oversight to the head of the Arcade. In addition, an Advisory Council, consisting of an equal number of representatives from the faculty, computing center and library, advises on all aspects of operations and policy, priorities and developments.

Although the administrative responsibility for the Information Arcade rests within the University Libraries, the essence of the facility continues to be a collaborative effort. In answer to a question from a colleague at another university, "how do you get the faculty to come to the Information Arcade," an Iowa librarian responded: "This was not difficult. They consider it their facility." There is little doubt that the early involvement of faculty in the development of the Information Arcade has contributed to its overwhelming success during its first year. In addition, it has provided an important opportunity for computing and library staff to work together in a totally different context, laying the foundation for future collaborative activities.

In fall semester 1992 as the Arcade opened, over twenty courses were taught fully or partially, despite the typical problems involved in the installation of computer workstations and the network. The spring 1993 semester has shown the same high level of use, with librarians now scheduling a variety of user education sessions in the Arcade as well. The use of the electronic classroom is now, after two semesters, at capacity. The focus for the Information Arcade will expand now to include a greater emphasis on working with faculty and students in the development of databases and exploring electronic resources, including the Internet, in support of research.

There is another aspect of this project that is worth noting. The academic computing center provides key support to faculty who need assistance in developing instructional, multimedia software through The Second Look Computing staff, who are specialist in this field. The director of this program has been involved in all aspects of the Information Arcade development, and there is a commitment by both groups to avoid duplication of effort and, instead, focus on how to complement one another in support of curriculum development.

The Information Arcade, in some manifestation, could be replicated on campuses across the country. Indeed, at the University of Iowa, we believe that the concept, though not necessarily the physical facility, of the Information Arcade needs to be replicated around the campus. More important, the collaborative effort among faculty, librarians and computer professionals for this project needs to be replicated in order to identify and provide the necessary support for integrating information technology into the curriculum.

Teaching Information Technology and Information Resources

The increasing importance of teaching as an essential element in the role of university libraries has been emphasized increasingly in the past several years. Librarians need to move beyond the limiting nature of bibliographic instruction to a more comprehensive concept of the "teaching library." This suggests a more active and involved role for librarians than the passive nature of reference desk service, and should transform the library from a focus on users coming to a facility to one in which services are constructed around the needs of individual users.

Traditionally, computing center staff also have had a role, though it may have been more of a minor key, in instructing computer users as well as providing assistance related to technology. The challenge is to find ways to combine the human resources and expertise of librarians and computer professionals in meeting a learning requirement of enormous magnitude among university faculty, students and staff, as they try to use information technology to its fullest potential. The capacity of information technology (whether for word processing, for building a research database, for electronic communication, or for accessing information sources) is not currently being exploited. Individuals lack the knowledge and skills to first find out what is available and possible, and then learn how to make the best use of resources to apply to their own work. Universities in varying degrees offer a treasure trove of technological "goodies," but too often leave faculty and students to struggle on their own to make full use of these resources.

On some campuses, professionals in the computer center and library are conducting parallel courses and, even in some instances, offering courses on the same subjects such as the Internet. The enormous task of training and providing support services for the university community in information technology will continue. Much more could be accomplished if the expertise of the two professionals groups were applied to address this challenge.

At Pennsylvania State University, staff from the Libraries and the Center for Academic Computing are combining their efforts to offer a monthly seminar on the uses and resources on the Internet. Nancy Cline, Dean of University Libraries, said that: "There is growing excitement throughout the University about the potential of the Internet. The Libraries — and our partners in academic computing — will be actively engaged in teaching users to make the most effective use of these emerging resources!"[25]

Additionally, librarians and computer professionals should be exploring the use of information technology to teach individuals about the technology. Librarians and computer professionals are encouraging faculty to redesign their courses using technology such as interactive multi-media and online interactive programs and distance delivery through satellite and fiber optic systems. It is time for the information professionals to use these same technologies in developing their own instructional programs.

For example, librarians and computer professionals could design a course instructing faculty and students in the use of the Internet using the network to conduct the class. This has already been done on a global basis when an individual conducted a session in how to navigate the system over the Internet with a worldwide enrollment in the tens of thousands. Even though a prerequisite was sufficient knowledge to get into the online system, there was an overwhelming response to this approach to learning the Internet.

In addition, librarians and computer professionals should work collaboratively to design stand-alone, computer-assisted instruction (CAI) packages for a wide range of basic and advanced instruction — orientation to the library system or computer resources, how to acquire and set up an electronic mail account, how to use a specific bibliographic source (print or electronic), and many other topics. Such CAI programs, or tutorials, could be available in a variety of formats, depending on the nature of the instructional package, including access on the campus network or the library online system, on stand-alone systems in conjunction with a particular location or information resource, and on floppy disks.

More advanced collaboration of professionals from the two organizations could explore establishing an entirely new model for services, such as that proposed on the library VISIONS listserv by Lipow.[26] This construct for "reference" assistance is based on a service found at Disney World. Characteristics of this service include remote user access via the "teledesk," which permits interactive visual and voice connections between the user and an Advisory Service Consultant — no longer "reference librarian." Developed on a campus, this model could offer individuals the ability to select whether they wish a technology or information specialists when they step up to a "teledesk" workstation.

The idea behind the "teledesk" is to maintain a level of personalized service in a distributed environment, one that is more efficient and more responsive than service at the current library or computer center information desk. This is not such a far-fetched idea, since the technology is available now.

Librarians and computer professionals have an enormous responsibility to find ways to transform services rather than only to offer efficiencies in delivery of information and the crunching of numbers. Unless education and research are improved, how will the payoff of the millions universities have invested in technology and information systems be demonstrated? When electronic systems for information delivery are created, but there is a failure to teach people how to make full use of these systems, only half the job is done.

Through collaborative approaches to assessment of the learning needs of faculty and students and to the design and delivery of instruction through a variety of means, computing and library professionals can transform their roles on campus and make a major contribution to the integration of information technology into improved education.

Electronic Publishing Within the University

Finally, a major endeavor that could be facilitated by librarians, technologists and faculty working collaboratively together at their institutions is to explore, through focused projects, the potential for the university to act as an electronic publisher of scholarly works. In a recent program involving university provosts, library directors, publishers and faculty, just such a project was identified as a priority to make available "electronic copies of texts in the public domain." The members of the group proposing this project indicated that such a "campus collaboration, involving initially the library and computing center, would provide leadership in helping other campus agencies, such as the university press, to enter more aggressively into the electronic publishing arena." [27]

Clearly this concept will never move beyond rhetoric unless some small group on a campus provides the leadership to initiate such a publishing venture. Again, computer and library professionals working together could act as the catalyst to initiate an electronic publishing project on their campus.

There are undoubtedly many other possible projects that computer and library professionals could work on that would make a needed contribution to the application of information technology to research, teaching and learning. All that is required is the willingness of individuals to step up to the task.

Conclusion

The changes brought about by information technology will continue to have a profound impact on organizational structure, working relationships, products and services. In the university there will be no department, function or activity that will go untouched. Professional staff in libraries and computer centers will surely be affected by these changes. And, if they choose, they can play a significant role in contributing to the shape of the university in the 21st century by providing leadership in the integration of information technology in thoughtful and innovative ways.

In a turbulent and rapidly changing environment, the contributions and the value of the role of computer and library professionals will be magnified if they pursue a strength in collaborative partnerships. It will not be an easy task either for individuals or for organizations, but it is one that will insure a creative and exciting future for information professionals into the 21st century.

Schrage provides the positive context for considering the personal and organizational advantage in selecting a collaborative model for work. He states that "the best of all possible collaborative futures offers a world where people can enjoy and indulge their individuality even as they enhance and augment their communities." 28

NOTES

1. Drucker, Peter F. "The New Society of Organizations," *Harvard Business Review* 70 (Sept-Oct 1992):95-96.

2. Higher Education Information Resources Alliance (HEIRA). "What Presidents Need to Know . . . about the Integration of Information Technologies on Campus." Boulder, CO: *CAUSE*, 1992. p.1.

3. Battin, Patricia. "The Electronic Library — A Vision for the Future," *EDUCOM Bulletin* 19, no. 2 (Summer 1984); Cimbala, Diane J. "The Scholarly Information Center: An Organizational Model," *College & Research Libraries* 48, no. 5 (Sept 1987); Molholt, Pat, "On Converging Paths: The Computing Center and the Library." *Journal of Academic Librarianship* 11.5 (Nov 1985); Neff, Raymond K. "Merging Libraries and Computer Centers: Manifest Destiny or Manifestly Deranged?" *EDUCOM Bulletin* 20, no. 4 (Winter 1985); Weber, David C. "University Libraries and Campus Information Technology Organizations: Who Is in Charge Here." *Journal of Library Administration* 9, no. 4. 1988.

4. Schrage, Michael. *Shared Minds: The New Technologies of Collaboration.* New York: Random House. 1990. p. 6.

5. Ibid, p.39.

6. Byrne, John A. "The Virtual Corporation." *Business Week* (February 8, 1993):99.

7. Association of Research Libraries. *The Emerging Virtual Research Library.* Washington, D.C.: Association of Research Libraries/Office of Management Services. 1992.

8. HEIRA, op. cit. p.2.

9. Neff, op.cit. p.8.

10. Molholt, op. cit. p.286.

11. Battin, op. cit. p.13.

12. Sack, John R. "Open Systems for Open Minds: Building the Library without Walls." *College & Research Libraries* 47, no. 6 (Nov 1986):536.

13. Jones, C. Lee. "Academic Libraries and Computing: A Time of Change." *EDUCOM Bulletin* 20, no. 1 (Spring 1985):10.

14. Dougherty, Richard M. "Libraries and Computing Centers: A Blueprint for Collaboration." *College & Research Libraries* 48, no. 4 (July 1987):293.

15. Creth, Sheila D. Notes from program conducted at Rutgers University, May 1991.

16. Battin, op. cit. p.12.

17. Keen, Peter G.W. "Redesigning the Organization Through Information Technology." *Planning Review* 19 (May/June 1991):5.

18. Ibid.

19. Drucker, op. cit. p.97-98.

20. Keen, op. cit. p.7.

21. Van Horn, Richard L. "How Significant is Computing for Higher Education." *EDUCOM Bulletin* 20, no. 1 (Spring 1985):7.

22. Creth, Sheila D. "Information Technology: Building a Framework for Change." *Library Issues* 12, no. 6 (July 1992):4.

23. Lucier, Richard E. "Toward a Knowledge Management Environment: A Strategic Framework." *EDUCOM Review* 27, no. 6 (Nov/Dec 1992):24.

24. Ibid. p.27.

25. Pennsylvania State University. Correspondence and materials from Nancy M. Cline, Dean, University Libraries. 1993.

26. Lipow, Anne. "21st century job description." VISIONS Listserv, August 1992.

27. Dougherty, Richard M. and Carol Hughes. *Preferred Library Futures II: Charting the Paths*. Mountain View, CA.: The Research Libraries Group, Inc. 1993. p. 16.

28. Schrage, op. cit. p.196.